ALSO BY AL ROKER

Don't Make Me Stop This Car!

Al Roker's Big Bad Book of Barbecue

AL ROKER'S
HASSLE-FREE
HOLIDAY COOKBOOK

*More Than 125 Recipes for Family
Celebrations All Year Long*

AL ROKER

RECIPES WRITTEN WITH MARIALISA CALTA

PHOTOGRAPHS BY MARK THOMAS

Scribner

NEW YORK LONDON TORONTO SYDNEY SINGAPORE

SCRIBNER

1230 Avenue of the Americas

New York, NY 10020

SCRIBNER and design are trademarks of Macmillan Library Reference USA, Inc.,

used under license by Simon & Schuster, the publisher of this work.

For information about special discounts for bulk purchases,

please contact Simon & Schuster Special Sales:

1-800-456-6798 or business@simonandschuster.com

Text set in Cantoria and Trade Gothic

Manufactured in the United States of America

1 3 5 7 9 10 8 6 4 2

Library of Congress Cataloging-in-Publication Data is available.

ISBN 0-7432-4952-6

Family is what the holidays are all about.
It's not a holiday unless you spend it with some family,
and family can be whatever you make it.

I'd like to dedicate this book to my family,
my source of strength and inspiration.
They are, in no particular order,
my mother, Isabel; my brother, Chris;
my sisters, Alisa, Desirée, and Patricia;
and my late father, Al, Sr.

Also I dedicate this book to my wife,
Deborah Roberts,
and my children, Courtney, Leila, and Nicholas.
Thank you for reminding me every day
about the most important things in life.
It really is all about you guys.

Acknowledgments

I'd like to thank my wonderful editor at Simon and Schuster, Trish Todd, who puts up with a lot of missed deadlines and is still one of the most pleasant people I know, as well as Beth Wareham and Rica Allannic at Scribner. Also a big tip of the tongs to my friend and representative, Alfred Geller, who gets things done and shares my passion for food. And to my assistant, Tekella Miller, who keeps me on track every day, or at least tries to.

Contents

Christmas Dinner   47

Christmas Brunch   67

Introduction

The Holidays. Those two words can strike terror into the heart of just about anybody. Why? Because not only does it mean family and friends are coming to your home, which, depending on the family and friends, can mean you're going to have the beginning of a nervous breakdown, it means you have to cook for them.

Now, if you're like me, you enjoy the chance to show off a bit. You wanna let 'em know that you can burn some pots.

On the other hand, you want to enjoy the holidays as well. You probably took some time off, thinking you'd kick back and relax. Now you're thinking that your home is going to be sacked by the Visigoths. You will be spending hours in the kitchen preparing huge sides of roast mutton and great roasts of beef, while your guests gorge themselves at long wooden tables by the massive stone fireplace and Great Danes gnaw on the bones the gluttons toss aside. Oh, I'm sorry. I was thinking of the Great Hall scene from *Robin Hood* when Errol Flynn tosses a dead deer at the feet of the Prince.

Anyway, fear not, forsooth and verily. That is why you purchased this book. My merry band of thieves take from the time-rich and give to the time-poor. Forget about taxing recipes! But enough of the Robin Hood theme.

I know what you're thinking. "Al, I don't need a cookbook for just Thanksgiving and Christmas! I entertain year-round!" Of course you do. This is a year-round holiday book, a book that can proudly sit out on your counter or under a small child to help him reach the table. Preferably one who's been potty trained. With this book, you can throw a party celebrating February 2nd, the day Punxsutawney Phil is hoisted from his burrow. I bet many is the time that you longed to rejoice on St. Lawrence's Day, feast of the patron Saint of barbecue, and now you can. Love to love Valentine's Day? We've got you covered. Ever hear of Boxing Day? Considering scaring up a party for Halloween? With these and so many other holidays in this book, you'll never be without an excuse to entertain.

We've presented a menu for each holiday, starting with appetizers and moving on to main courses, sides, and desserts. We even have cool, refreshing beverages if the season calls for it, or hot, comforting drinks if that's what the calendar indicates.

To accomplish this feat of cookbook derring-do, I had help. Marialisa Calta is a recipe writer par excellence and a darn good cook in her own right. We teamed up a couple of years ago for *Al Roker's Big Bad Book of Barbecue*. She took the recipes that I had gathered over the years from my own backyard cookouts, friends, and family and massaged them. Before I met Marialisa, my basic M.O. was a handful of this and a pinch of that. Measuring cup? We don' need no stinkin' measuring cup!

Actually, we did. Otherwise, how would people know how much of what to use? So Marialisa refined the recipes and then, more importantly, tested them to make sure nobody keeled over.

Since this book is a little more wide-ranging, we collaborated a lot more. We spent a lot of time talking about what kind of food I cooked and when, the holidays my family celebrates, and what we ate, both as kids and now as adults.

Then we put together the menus and themes for the holidays. Some menus are direct throwbacks to childhood, and others reflect what we like to devour now. Still others represent what we'd *like* to set on the table.

As you know when you cook for the holidays, it takes real skill to be able to come up with food that not only tastes good but is interesting and not a pain in the keester to make. While Marialisa and I were developing the recipes, we felt it was important to keep things as hassle-free as possible. In fact, this book is intended to help you actually enjoy yourself at your own holiday gatherings.

This ain't America in the 1950s and 1960s. In those days, our mothers were mostly at home, taking care of the kids and making sure the family was well fed. It was hard to prepare for a holiday then, but it's even harder now, with both parents working and children whose after-school schedules can resemble the flow chart of a major corporation. Maybe you have your parties catered, complete with white-jacketed servers passing trays of canapés to your family and friends. But if you're like me, you and your significant other are running around like maniacs to get everything ready—cook, set the table, make the drinks—*and* visit with the people you invited and intended to be with in the first place.

There was a time when I wanted to do everything. From appetizers to dessert, I had to be in control. And I was. I was also missing out on being at my own party, whether it was a brunch or a sit-down dinner. I've learned that being in control is a hassle. I have learned that my best, most fun parties are hassle-free.

I don't have to make everything from scratch. I can purchase prepeeled garlic cloves. I can use bagged spinach or lettuce (I still wash it no matter what the bag says), and I have learned to appreciate ready-made pie crusts.

And guess what? If I invite you over, don't ask, "Can I bring anything?" if you don't mean it. That's because I *will* take you up on it. See, that's using the hassle-free philosophy. If you make a better apple pie than I do, why would I waste time trying to make that pie when you can bring it? One less thing for me to do.

My mother, Isabel Roker, worked miracles during the traditional holidays. With only one oven and a four-burner cooktop, she would churn out two meats, several vegetables, mashed potatoes, and a baked macaroni, effortlessly. Well, it seemed effortless. Now I know why she only weighs about 100 pounds. She was juggling pots, roasting pans, and baking dishes, putting the guy who spun the plates on the *Ed Sullivan Show* to shame.

But my mother was no control freak; she would enlist us kids to help out. Potatoes to peel, green beans to cut, dishes to set out? She got us involved. Helping mom became part of our family tradition. Involving your family is the best hassle-free strategy of all. Not only does it give you a break, it allows you to spend time together. Remember . . . you don't have to do it all yourself. And so what if it isn't done exactly the way you'd do it? No one will know if you don't tell. Hassle-free, baby.

From St. Patrick's Day to Halloween to the Fourth of July, we love any excuse to get together. You can take advantage of them all if you live by the hassle-free philosophy.

This book is full of recipes, shortcuts, tips, and strategies that can make entertaining for any holiday as easy as possible.

Do not fear the holidays. Together we can look at a holiday on the calendar and say, "Bring it on! Do your worst! I am ready for you." I do, however, draw the line at talking to your Aunt Millie, the one who's got the fuzzy lip thing going. You're on your own with her.

AL ROKER'S
HASSLE-FREE
HOLIDAY COOKBOOK

Thanksgiving with All the Trimmings

Thanksgiving is my favorite holiday of the year. Why? Because it's just you, your family, and a large bird. There are no presents, no pine needles on the floor, and no staying up overnight trying to put bicycles together (because Santa forgot). On Thanksgiving, the object of the game is to end up on the couch in the living room, top button of your pants undone, zipper at half-mast, and head lolling to the side in a tryptophan-induced stupor.

When I was growing up in Queens, our Thanksgiving started early in the morning. Because we had only one oven, my mom would get up early and start on the side dishes. By the time we kids stumbled downstairs, the turkey was already in the oven, the Macy's Thanksgiving Day Parade was on TV, and breakfast was on the table. After breakfast, Mom put out a bowl of fruit and nuts for us to snack on so that we wouldn't come into the kitchen and disrupt her. Her Thanksgiving dinner was as highly choreographed as the Radio City Music Hall Christmas Spectacular.

Now my mom wasn't exactly relaxed in the Thanksgiving kitchen, but I know now she held the key to a hassle-free holiday: She was just plain organized. She went food shopping with a list. The night before, she prepped a lot of stuff that she could reheat quickly after the turkey came out of the oven. She asked people who were coming to bring certain items. It was important to her that everything be fresh. Yes, she could've saved time with frozen green beans, but instead she delegated responsibility. After all, she had six little prep chefs available to her. Okay, maybe not my baby brother, Chris. He was special. He didn't have to do chores . . . So I have issues. I'm working on it!

I learned about delegation from my mom. Generally, I'm the one in charge of the kitchen, especially on holidays. However, on Thanksgiving Day, I'm working. As one of the hosts for Macy's Thanksgiving Day Parade on NBC, I'm in Herald Square watching a giant Garfield float by.

I can't be home to make sure the turkey hits the oven early and certain dishes are prepped and started. My wife, Deborah gets involved, as does my mother. Last year was my daughter Leila's first year helping prep the meal. She was the official food master. Delegation is our new Thanksgiving tradition. I gotta tell you, it's nice walking into my warm house and smelling turkey roasting and sweet potatoes baking.

For your Thanksgiving dinner, get people to bring ready-made dishes for each course, from appetizers to desserts. I do think it would be a bit cheeky to ask someone to bring a turkey, but hey, you never know. Keep appetizers simple. Serve everyone food that even the kids will like, no separate dishes for them. The weekend before Thanksgiving, make some things that you can refrigerate or freeze until Turkey Day.

Go shopping with a list, set the table the night before, and make sure you have enough plates, glasses, and flatware.

Ladies and gentlemen, preheat your ovens.

Creamy Mushroom Soup

Who doesn't love Cream of Mushroom soup? It is comfort in a can. The familiar red and white with recipes on the side has been a boon to many a harried housewife. Take Cream of Mushroom soup, frozen green beans, and French-fried onions and voilà: a casserole that a vegetarian could love.

Here's a chance to make your own MMMM! MMMM! MMMMMM! pretty darn good mushroom soup.

⅓ cup extra-virgin olive oil
1 large onion, peeled and finely chopped
3 cloves garlic, peeled and finely chopped
⅓ cup all-purpose flour
3 pounds button mushrooms, wiped clean and thinly sliced
4 teaspoons chopped sage leaves, or 1½ teaspoons dried sage

4 teaspoons thyme leaves, or 1½ teaspoons dried thyme, plus extra for serving
1 bay leaf
Salt
Freshly ground pepper
2 quarts whole milk
3 tablespoons dry cooking sherry, optional

---

1 • Warm the oil in a large pot over medium-high heat until hot but not smoking. Add the onion and garlic and cook, stirring, for 5 minutes, until softened but not browned. Add the flour and cook, stirring, for 2 to 3 minutes. Stir in the mushrooms, sage, thyme, and bay leaf and season generously with salt and pepper. Reduce the heat to low, cover the pot, and simmer until the mushrooms start to soften and give up some of their liquid, about 5 minutes. Stir in the milk and cook, stirring occasionally, until the soup is hot throughout, about 10 minutes. Add the sherry, if using, cover, and simmer gently for at least 15 minutes more, until the mushrooms are very tender. Do not allow the soup to boil.

2 • The soup can be cooled in a bowl, covered, and refrigerated for up to 24 hours or frozen in an airtight container for up to 1 month. If frozen, allow the soup to thaw, then reheat over medium-low heat, stirring occasionally, until very hot.

3 • Ladle the soup into 8 warm soup bowls and garnish with a sprinkling of thyme.

Makes about 12 cups, or 8 servings

Stocking the Holiday Pantry and Freezer

You'll be doing more baking at this time of year, so stock up on extra flour, sugar, nuts, baking chocolate, butter, and frozen fruit or cans of fruit or pie filling. Nuts and butter can be kept for weeks in the freezer, and frozen fruit does triple duty as a dessert, pie filling, or ice cream topping. Check your supply and the expiration dates of baking powder and baking soda (see page 79 for quick freshness tests) and make sure you have enough vanilla and almond extracts, ground cinnamon, ginger, nutmeg and molasses on hand. Stock up on colored sugars, sprinkles, and other cookie decorations, including chocolate chips and raisins. If you never get around to making cookies, they're good for 2 A.M. pantry raids. Stash a package or two of store-bought puff pastry in the freezer; it can be used to make tarts (page 46) and hors d'oeuvres (pages 8–9), among other things. For hassle-free pies, keep some refrigerated, prepared pie crusts on hand—they freeze well, too. Ice cream makes an instant dessert; dress it up with Chocolate Sauce (page 155). Consider making double batches of your favorite dishes and freezing them for later use. (Unless, of course, my family comes over. Then double batches might just cover it.)

Holidays are crunch time in the kitchen. So don't feel guilty about buying supplies that help you take shortcuts, including precut vegetables, pitted olives, canned beans, shredded cheeses, and bottled sauces.

Look, I like "from scratch" as much as the next guy, but if I have to choose between spending time with friends and spending time slicing, dicing, and chopping, I'll take the friends anytime. Forgive me, Mom.

For last-minute entertaining, keep emergency supplies on hand. Keep them in a case with a hammer and a glass door that says "Break in Case of Last-Minute Guests" (see Ten Things to Put on a Cracker, page 118). Essential emergency supplies include crackers, cans of smoked oysters or mussels, olives, and pickles. The Antipasti

Salad (page 217) can be entirely assembled from pantry products. Freeze smoked salmon, cheeses, and sliced deli meats; thaw in the refrigerator for several hours (or overnight) before serving.

If you have room in your freezer, store a loaf of crusty French or Italian bread; wrap it in foil and warm it in a 350°F oven for about 15 minutes before serving.

Potato Leek Soup

I really like this soup. I've eaten it as a meal by itself. A good hunk of crusty bread and a bowl of this soup and you're set. It's also a nice starter for a cold-weather holiday meal.

4 tablespoons (½ stick) unsalted butter
3 large leeks (2¼ pounds), trimmed, cut into ½-inch pieces, rinsed well, and dried
2 medium onions, peeled and cut into ½-inch pieces
3 cloves garlic, peeled and finely chopped

1½ pounds Yukon gold or other yellow potatoes (about 4 medium), peeled and cut into 1½-inch chunks
3 (14-ounce) cans chicken broth
Salt
Freshly ground pepper
3 cups half-and-half or 2 (12-ounce) cans evaporated milk
Chopped chives, for serving

1 • Melt the butter in a large pot over medium heat. Add the leeks, onions, and garlic and cook, stirring, until they begin to soften, about 5 minutes. Add the potatoes and cook, stirring occasionally, for 5 minutes longer. Add the broth, season with salt and pepper, and cover the pot. Bring to a boil over high heat, reduce the heat, and simmer until the potatoes can be easily pierced with a knife, 15 to 20 minutes.

2 • Working in batches, puree the soup in a blender or food processor until very smooth. The soup can be cooled in a bowl, covered, and refrigerated for up to 2 days or frozen in an airtight container for up to 1 month. If frozen, thaw before proceeding.

3 • Return the soup to the pot, place over medium-low heat, and add the half-and-half. Stir occasionally until the soup is very hot, but do not allow it to boil.

4 • Ladle the soup into 8 warm soup bowls and garnish with the chopped chives.

Makes about 12 cups, or 8 servings

NOTE: This soup can also be served cold.

VARIATION

Carrot Leek Soup

Substitute 1½ pounds carrots for the potatoes.

No-Cook Hors d'Oeuvres for a Crowd

A lot of food's about to hit the table, so you don't want folks filling up before it's served. But you need to serve something that will stave off the ravenous and buy you a bit of extra time for putting those finishing touches on the feast. To keep snackers out of the kitchen, set out an old-fashioned "relish tray"—celery sticks, olives and radishes—with some updated additions to whet the appetite.

- *Check the condiment aisle of your supermarket for olives stuffed with slivers of almonds, with garlic, and with jalapeño peppers. Also check out the imported, brine-cured and oil-cured black olives.*
- *Pickles—whether pickled cucumbers or other vegetables—add tang and crunch to your pre-dinner offerings. Your supermarket is likely to carry jars of pickled carrots, pickled asparagus, pickled green beans, and pickled okra.*
- *Bowls of mini carrots, broccoli florets, and vegetable sticks (zucchini, fresh cucumbers, celery, and slices of red, yellow, and green bell peppers) are colorful additions to the before-dinner spread. Peel and cut them ahead of time and refrigerate them in plastic bags. You can serve them as-is, or with simple dips such as Blue Cheese Dressing (page 53) or Mustard-Mayo Sauce or Chile-Mayo Sauce (page 206).*
- *Serve radishes with softened unsalted butter (page 25) and coarse sea salt for dipping. The butter tones down the sharp flavor of the radish.*
- *Offer a selection of nuts. Toasted almonds, pistachios, cashews, and macadamias are especially festive.*
- *Slices of Italian or French bread, focaccia or other flatbreads are great for dipping. Pour some fruity, extra-virgin olive oil into bowls and season it, if you like, with chopped garlic, salt, and chopped herbs such as basil, oregano, rosemary, or thyme.*

- *Arrange a platter with fresh figs or slices of cantaloupe wrapped with thin slices of prosciutto or smoked ham.*
- *Selections of dried fruits—apricots, apples, pineapple—are attractive and tasty.*

Thanksgiving Salad with Parsley Dressing

Bless my Mom. Every Thanksgiving, she would make a salad. Now, there's only so much room on your plate for food. When I was a kid, my feeling was, why waste valuable plate real estate on salad, when there's ham and sweet potatoes to be had? But I'm older now, and more health conscious . . . So this one's for you, Mom.

FOR THE DRESSING

½ cup packed parsley leaves
2 cloves garlic, peeled and halved
¼ cup lemon juice (from 1 to 2 lemons)
1 teaspoon dried dill

½ teaspoon celery seeds
½ teaspoon salt
½ teaspoon sugar
½ cup canola or other vegetable oil

In a blender, combine the parsley, garlic, and lemon juice and blend until smooth. Add the dill, celery seed, salt, and sugar and puree again. With the motor running, pour the oil in slowly, so that it is incorporated into the dressing and creates an emulsion. Cover and refrigerate for at least 30 minutes or up to 2 days.

FOR THE SALAD

12 cups mixed lettuces, such as red leaf,
green leaf and baby spinach
(6 ounces)
6 scallions, white and green parts, chopped
½ cup dried cranberries

1 cup sliced almonds or chopped
pecans, toasted (page 23)
2 pears or tart apples (such as
Granny Smiths), cored and cut
into ¼-inch pieces

Put the greens in a bowl and sprinkle the remaining ingredients on top. Just before serving, add the dressing and toss to coat the ingredients.

Makes 8 servings

Festive Juice Drinks

Juice has it all: color, sweetness, fresh taste, and the ability to blend well with other flavors. Kids love it straight or mixed with seltzer or soda water. Adults love juice straight or mixed with almost anything but rubbing alcohol. A touch of rum, bourbon, vodka, or gin can perk up a glass of juice right nicely.

If you have a juicer, go to town. But canned and bottled juice and concentrates will serve you well, especially if you are entertaining a crowd. Below are some winning combinations; serve them over plenty of ice, and decorate them, if you'd like, with slices of lemons, limes, or oranges; frozen raspberries or strawberries; or maraschino cherries. For glassware, you can go plain with a set of canning jars or plastic cups, or fancy with champagne flutes. Add some jazzy straws and swizzle sticks for fun.

- *Equal parts chilled grape juice, orange juice, and seltzer.*
- *One part chilled cranberry juice cocktail to 2 parts chilled ginger ale or champagne.*
- *Equal parts chilled apple juice, cranberry juice, and lemon-lime soda.*
- *Two parts chilled pineapple juice, 1 part chilled orange juice, 1 part chilled, brewed black tea with sugar and a squeeze of lemon.*
- *Equal parts chilled grape juice and lemon-lime soda.*
- *Equal parts chilled orange juice, apple juice, and seltzer.*
- *Equal parts chilled orange juice, pink grapefruit juice, and pineapple juice.*

Roast Turkey and Gravy

I never had to carve a turkey before my dad passed away. That's not to say that he didn't hack up the turkey as much as the next guy. It just wasn't my problem. Recently I've been boning up (pardon the pun) on carving. I've talked with several experts and a knife thrower about how to carve a turkey, but it's really not that complicated.

Once the bird is out of the oven, let it rest on a carving board for fifteen to twenty minutes, covered loosely with foil. Then, start by finding the breast-bone. Stick a two-pronged fork into the breast to steady the turkey. Take a sharp carving knife and—starting at the neck—slice down and into one breast along the breast bone. When you can't cut anymore, slice a horizontal cut halfway across the turkey. That allows you to lift out one half of the breast white meat. Then repeat that on the other side of the breastbone. Cut the two breast halves into thin slices. As for the legs, wiggle each leg, locate the joint, and cut the legs free from the body before slicing.

We've all heard the fun police say not to roast your turkey with the stuffing in it. Botulism, salmonella, and cooties could bring everyone to their knees. I am stating for insurance purposes, roast your turkey unstuffed. All right, now that I've satisfied the lawyers, I confess that I like the stuffing in the turkey. I've been eating stuffed turkey for probably forty-seven of my forty-nine years on earth, and neither I nor anyone I know has ever gotten sick. You just need to make sure the stuffing reaches at least 160°F. That's the big secret. So put the stuffing in a casserole dish instead if you're the nervous type. Otherwise, have at it!

FOR THE TURKEY

1 (14- to 16-pound) fresh turkey or thawed frozen turkey	Stuffing of your choice (pages 20–23)
Salt	About 8 tablespoons (1 stick) unsalted butter, melted
Freshly ground pepper	1 cup dry white wine

1 • Position a rack in the oven so that the turkey—in a roasting pan—will fit inside. Preheat the oven to 325°F. Remove the neck and giblets from the body cavities of the turkey. Rinse the turkey inside and out under cold running water, drain, and pat dry inside and out with paper towels. Season both the body cavity and the neck cavity with salt and pepper.

2 • Stuff the turkey just before you are going to put it in the oven: Spoon some of the stuffing into the neck cavity and pull the neck skin to cover it, securing the skin to the body of the turkey with the thin metal pins sold in supermarkets for this purpose. Lightly spoon more stuffing into the body cavity; but do not pack it in. (Place any remaining stuffing in a buttered baking dish, cover with foil, and refrigerate until needed.)

3 • To close the body cavity, tuck the drumsticks under the band of skin across the tail end, or into the heatproof plastic or metal bracket that comes with some turkeys. If your turkey has neither a band of skin nor a bracket, simply tie the drumsticks together with kitchen string.

4 • Brush the entire turkey with about 4 tablespoons of the melted butter. Sprinkle generously with salt and pepper. Place the turkey, breast side up, in a roasting pan with sides at least 2 inches high. (If you can, place the turkey on a roasting rack—a wire cake rack will do—to keep the turkey from sticking to the bottom of the pan.) Cover the breast and the meaty part of the drumsticks with a piece of heavy-duty aluminum foil to prevent overbrowning.

5 • Roast the turkey for 15 to 18 minutes per pound, or between 3½ hours and 4 hours and 15 minutes for a 14-pound turkey and between 4 hours and 4 hours and 50 minutes for a 16-pound turkey. Baste the turkey every 30 to 40 minutes with the butter and other juices that collect at the bottom of the pan; lift the foil to get at the breast and brush on a bit more of the remaining melted butter each time. If you are using a self-basting turkey, you don't have to baste it (but it doesn't hurt).

6 • About an hour before you estimate the turkey will be done, remove the foil, and pour the wine into the pan. Continue to roast until the built-in thermometer pops up, or a meat thermometer—or an instant-read thermometer—inserted in the thigh registers 180°F to 185°F. If at any time during this last period of roasting the breast or drumsticks appear to be overbrowning, cover them again with aluminum foil.

7 • When the turkey is done, remove it from the oven and transfer it to a cutting board. Reserve the pan drippings in the roasting pan. Check the temperature of the stuffing: for safety reasons, it should register at least 160°F. If the stuffing is done, spoon it into a

serving dish and cover to keep warm. If the stuffing needs additional cooking, transfer it to a buttered baking dish and return it to the oven. (If you had leftover stuffing when you stuffed the turkey, now is the time to put that dish, covered, into the oven; bake for about 30 minutes until hot.) Cover the turkey with a large piece of aluminum foil and let rest for 15 to 20 minutes before carving; make the gravy while it rests.

FOR THE GRAVY

Pan drippings from turkey
Canned chicken broth (up to 4 cups)
1/4 cup all-purpose flour

1 to 2 tablespoons dry white wine or
  dry cooking sherry, optional
Salt
Freshly ground pepper

1 • Pour the reserved pan drippings from the turkey roasting pan into a 4-cup glass measure, bowl, or gravy separator. Allow the drippings to stand for a few minutes so that the fat floats to the top. Skim off all of the fat and reserve only 1/4 cup. Reserve the pan juices in the glass measure.

2 • Set the roasting pan over 2 burners and warm over low heat, adding 1 cup of broth to the pan and stirring to scrape up the little browned bits stuck to the bottom. After a minute or two, when you have thoroughly deglazed the pan, pour the contents into the container holding the pan juices. You need 4 cups of liquid; add enough chicken broth to reach the desired amount.

3 • In a medium saucepan, mix the reserved 1/4 cup turkey fat with the flour over low heat, whisking constantly. Slowly whisk in the 4 cups liquid. When all of the liquid is incorporated, add the wine, if desired. Simmer, whisking constantly, until the gravy thickens, about 10 minutes. Season with salt and pepper. Keep warm over very low heat until needed, or for up to 1 hour.

4 • Carve the turkey, and arrange the slices on a warm platter. Drizzle with warm gravy, and pass the extra gravy in a sauceboat.

Makes 14 to 16 servings

NOTE: If you choose to roast the turkey without stuffing, you will want to add the following to the body cavity to flavor the turkey from the inside out and keep it moist: 1 onion, peeled and quartered; 2 cloves garlic, peeled and halved; 1 lemon, halved; 1 stalk celery, cut into chunks; several bay leaves and a few sprigs parsley. Roast an unstuffed turkey for 12 to 15 minutes per pound, until the built-in thermometer pops up, or a meat thermometer—or an instant-read thermometer—inserted in the thigh registers 180°F to 185°F.

Turkey Basics

Let's get up close and personal with your holiday bird.

FRESH OR FROZEN?

There are advantages to both, really. Fresh turkeys are all-natural and can go from fridge to oven with little thought. But you can't buy them weeks ahead of the big day, like you can frozen turkeys. With all the last-minute errands and cooking, you might just appreciate having the main event safely nestled in your freezer well in advance. Just remember to start defrosting it three to four days in advance (see opposite).

MY FAVORITE BIRD

Let's face it: We've all had a dried-out, tough, stringy turkey at least once in our lives. You know, the kind you need to eat with a quart of cranberry sauce just to get it down? Brining—soaking the turkey in salty water overnight in the refrigerator—is the perfect way to get a juicy, moist bird. The problem is that this time of year there just isn't enough room in my refrigerator for a five-gallon pail.

The solution? A pre-brined, self-basting turkey. Most grocery stores carry them. The soaking step has been done for you so you get all the benefits of brining without having to do it yourself. Plus, the turkey is self-basting, meaning you won't have to reach into the oven every 30 minutes to baste the beast (unless of course you want to). This is one of my favorite hassle-free tips.

TURKEY MATH

Figure about a pound per person, fresh or frozen. This will provide generous servings and leave plenty of leftovers (see page 18 for recipe ideas to use up extras).

DEFROSTING A FROZEN TURKEY

First and foremost, do not thaw a turkey at room temperature.

To thaw a frozen turkey, put the still-wrapped turkey, breast side up, on a rimmed tray, transfer it to the refrigerator, and allow it to thaw for one day per four pounds of turkey, or about four days for a sixteen-pound bird.

If you forgot to thaw your turkey ahead of time, you can defrost a turkey by putting it—still in its wrapper—breast down in a bucket or sink and covering it completely with cold water. Change the water every thirty minutes, draining the turkey completely and adding more cold water. It will take at least thirty minutes per pound of turkey to defrost, or at least eight hours for a sixteen-pound bird. As soon as it is thawed, refrigerate the bird until you are ready to stuff and roast. This is not a hassle-free alternative, unless you have a full-time turkey assistant, so remember to thaw your bird ahead of time.

IS IT DINNER YET?

A stuffed turkey will take approximately fifteen to eighteen minutes per pound to cook, or four to nearly five hours for a sixteen-pound turkey. An unstuffed turkey needs twelve to fifteen minutes per pound in the oven. Roast your turkey until the built-in thermometer pops up, or a meat thermometer—or an instant-read thermometer—inserted in the thigh registers 180°F to 185°F. Remember to check the temperature of the stuffing, too: it should register at least 160°F. If it doesn't, but the turkey is done, spoon the stuffing into a buttered baking dish and return it to the oven while the turkey rests.

IF ALL ELSE FAILS . . .

If the cooking pro in your family (mom, cousin, brother) can't be reached (on a plane, at the hairdresser, still doesn't have a cell phone) right when you have an important question, do not despair. See page 263 for Holiday Hotlines, many staffed by real, live kitchen experts waiting to help.

Turkey Leftovers

No matter how hard my family tries (and believe me, we do try), we can never devour all that is on the Thanksgiving table in one sitting. I bet we're not the only ones. But turkey-day leftovers make great meals—and I'm talking way beyond the standard-issue turkey sandwich here (see below for recipes)—for days to come. For safety reasons, aim to have leftovers in the refrigerator no more than two hours after they come out of the oven. Carve extra turkey off the bone, refrigerate just until cool, then wrap and return to the fridge for up to three days, or freeze for up to about a month.

To make sure leftover casseroles that you're reheating are hot all the way through, insert a metal knife into the center and leave it there for about 15 seconds. Remove the knife and carefully touch the back of your hand with the flat part of the knife. If the knife is hot, so are the leftovers.

CREAMED TURKEY

Melt 4 tablespoons (½ stick) unsalted butter in a medium saucepan over medium heat. Whisk in ¼ cup all-purpose flour and cook, whisking, until the mixture is smooth, about 3 minutes. Gradually whisk in one 14-ounce can chicken broth, and a small, grated, peeled onion. Season with salt and pepper. Cook for about 10 minutes, stirring occasionally, until the mixture is beginning to bubble but does not boil. Add 4 cups diced, cooked turkey and stir to mix well. Cook for a few more minutes until the turkey is heated through. Serve over cooked egg noodles and sprinkle with snipped chives or chopped parsley, if desired. Makes 4 servings.

QUICK TURKEY POT PIE

Make creamed turkey (above) and stir in 3 to 4 cups frozen (and thawed) mixed vegetables. Turn into a buttered, 3- or 4-quart baking dish and top with an unbaked, store-bought, 9-inch pie crust, or with Baking Powder Biscuit dough (page 28), dropping the dough in spoonfuls over the top. Bake in a preheated, 400°F oven for 30 to 40 minutes, until the crust is golden and the filling is bubbling. Makes 6 servings.

CURRIED TURKEY SALAD

Mix 3 cups diced, cooked turkey with 1½ cups halved seedless white grapes, 1 stalk chopped celery, and chopped red onion to taste. Stir in ½ cup sliced almonds, if desired. In a small bowl, mix together ¾ cup mayonnaise, 1 teaspoon curry powder, 2 teaspoons lemon juice, and a dash of soy sauce. Toss the mayonnaise mixture with the turkey mixture. Serve on a plate or in a sandwich. Makes 4 servings.

Basic Bread Stuffing

I love stuffing. It is my favorite part of the Thanksgiving meal, especially the stuffing that cooked with the bird. Is it low-calorie? Heck no. Is it tasty? Heck YEAH!!!! There as many different styles of stuffing as there are people serving it. I'm including some variations, but this is my favorite. Basic. Fattening. Gone!

6 tablespoons (¾ stick) unsalted butter
2 medium onions, peeled and cut into
   ½-inch pieces
2 stalks celery, trimmed and cut into
   ½-inch pieces
2 cloves garlic, peeled and coarsely
   chopped
½ cup chopped parsley leaves
3 tablespoons chopped herbs, such as
   sage, basil, oregano, and thyme,
   or 1½ tablespoons dried herbs

Salt
Freshly ground pepper
8 cups homemade bread cubes (see
   opposite) or croutons (page 69),
   1 (14-ounce) bag store-bought
   stuffing or 2 (6-ounce) boxes
   store-bought croutons
1 to 2 cups canned chicken broth

1 • Melt the butter in a saucepan over medium heat. Add the onions, celery, and garlic and cook, stirring, until softened but not browned, about 5 minutes. Remove from the heat. Stir in the parsley and herbs and season with salt and pepper.

2 • Place the bread cubes in a large bowl and stir in the onion mixture. The stuffing can be covered and refrigerated for up to 2 days.

3 • Just before you stuff the turkey, add enough broth to moisten the stuffing without making it soggy. Stir well.

Makes about 12 cups stuffing, or enough for a 14- to 16-pound turkey

NOTE: If you want to cook the stuffing outside of the turkey, put it in two 9-inch square buttered baking dishes, dot with 1 to 2 tablespoons unsalted butter, and moisten with about ⅓ cup additional chicken broth. Cover and bake for 25 to 30 minutes in a preheated 325°F oven, until heated through.

VARIATIONS

Choose one or more, according to your taste and what you have on hand.

Vegetables

Sauté up to 2 cups diced carrots, mushrooms, leeks, or fennel along with the onions, celery, and garlic.

Nuts

Chop up to 2 cups toasted pecans, walnuts, pine nuts, hazelnuts, or almonds (for toasting instructions, see page 23) and stir them in just before you add the broth. You can also use roasted and shelled fresh chestnuts, or frozen or canned (but not packed in syrup) chestnuts.

Dried fruit

Stir in up to 2 cups diced dried apples, apricots, or prunes, or whole dried cherries or cranberries just before you add the broth.

Fresh fruit

Stir in up to 2 cups diced apples or pears just before you add the broth.

Liquids

Substitute apple cider, apple juice, orange juice, white wine, or canned vegetable broth for all or part of the chicken broth.

TO MAKE HOMEMADE BREAD CUBES: Slice a 1-pound loaf of bread (white, whole wheat, multigrain, Italian, or French) and lay the slices out in a single layer on baking sheets; let sit overnight to dry out. Cut into ¼-inch pieces. A 1-pound loaf will yield 8 cups of bread cubes.

Corn Bread Stuffing for a Crowd

A lot of folks like corn bread stuffing, but it is not hassle-free, or so I used to think. First you have to make corn bread, then you have to make stuffing. I used to avoid making it until it dawned on me that I could *buy* a dozen corn muffins. Presto: no more hassle! You won't be able to tell the difference and you'll save some time as well. Of course, if you're a stickler for the home-made variety, be my guest.

Corn and Cheese Muffins (page 137), 12 store-bought corn muffins, or a 9 by 5-inch loaf corn bread (store-bought or made from a mix)
1 pound hot or mild Italian sausage, removed from casings
Unsalted butter
2 medium onions, peeled and cut into ½-inch pieces
3 stalks celery, trimmed and cut into ½-inch pieces
1 green bell pepper, stemmed, seeded, and cut into ½-inch pieces
1 red bell pepper, stemmed, seeded, and cut into ½-inch pieces
1 cup chopped parsley leaves

1 tablespoon chopped sage leaves, or 1 teaspoon dried sage
1 tablespoon thyme leaves, or 1 teaspoon dried thyme
1 tablespoon chopped rosemary leaves, or 1 teaspoon dried rosemary, optional
½ teaspoon hot red pepper flakes, optional
1½ cups chopped pecans, toasted (see opposite)
Salt
Freshly ground pepper
About 1 cup canned chicken broth or apple cider

1 • Preheat the broiler with the rack set 5 to 6 inches from the heat source. Cut the corn muffins or corn bread into 1½-inch chunks, scatter them on a baking sheet, and toast them under the broiler, turning once, until they begin to brown, about 5 minutes. Set aside.

2 • Warm a large pot over medium heat. Add the sausage, break it into pieces with a spoon, and cook, stirring occasionally, until well browned, 12 to 15 minutes. Using a slotted spoon, transfer the sausage to a plate and set it aside.

3 • Measure the fat left in the pan—you want about ½ cup. If needed, add butter to make ½ cup. Add the onions, celery, and bell peppers and cook, stirring, until softened, 8 to 10 minutes. Add the parsley, sage, thyme, rosemary, and red pepper flakes, if using. Stir in the pecans and the toasted corn bread. Season with salt and pepper, and stir well. Use immediately or cool, cover, and refrigerate for up to 2 days. Allow the stuffing to come to room temperature before proceeding.

4 • Preheat the oven to 325°F.

5 • Just before you stuff the turkey, add enough broth to moisten the stuffing without making it soggy. Stir well.

6 • Stuff the turkey (page 13). Butter a 9-inch square baking dish and spoon the remaining stuffing in it. (If you're cooking all of the stuffing outside the turkey, you'll need three 9-inch buttered baking dishes.) Dot with 1 to 2 tablespoons unsalted butter and moisten with about ⅓ cup additional broth. Cover and bake for 25 to 30 minutes in a preheated 325°F oven, until the stuffing is heated through.

Makes about 18 cups stuffing, or enough to stuff a 14- to 16- pound turkey and fill a 9-inch square baking dish as well

TO TOAST NUTS: Preheat the oven to 350°F. Place shelled nuts in a single layer in an ovenproof skillet and toast, stirring occasionally, until fragrant and beginning to brown, about 10 minutes. You can also toast nuts in a skillet over medium-high heat, stirring frequently. Or place the nuts on a layer of paper towels on a microwave-safe plate and microwave on high power for 2 to 3 minutes. (The time will vary according to the size and power of your microwave oven.) Whatever method you use, keep an eye on the nuts; they go from brown to black pretty quickly.

Higher Stuffing Math

For turkeys over 10 pounds, figure you'll use about ¾ cup of stuffing per pound of turkey. Smaller turkeys, under 10 pounds, will need only ½ cup per pound.

Sweet Potato Poon

This is a favorite in the Roker household. My mother's been making this for as long as I can remember. It's like a crustless, sweet potato pie topped with browned marshmallows. Tradition dictates that one of us distract Mom when she puts the poon covered with marshmallows under the broiler to toast the marshmallows. Every year while she's standing in front of the oven with the broiler door open, browning the marshmallows, somebody asks her a question. She forgets about the poon and before you know it, the marshmallows catch fire and all hell breaks loose. Every year, the same thing. Look, we're easily amused. It's the holidays.

6 large sweet potatoes (about
    4 pounds), peeled and cut into
    1-inch chunks
1 cup all-purpose flour
4 teaspoons baking powder
1 teaspoon salt
1 teaspoon ground cinnamon
1 teaspoon ground nutmeg

1 teaspoon ground allspice
8 tablespoons (1 stick) unsalted
    butter, softened (see opposite)
    and cut into chunks
1 cup packed dark brown sugar
1 (8-ounce) can crushed pineapple,
    drained
1 (10-ounce) bag large marshmallows

1 • Pour 2 to 3 inches of water into a large pot and bring to a boil. Set the sweet potatoes in a steamer basket over the boiling water, taking care not to let the potatoes sit in the water. Cover and steam the sweet potatoes until they can be easily pierced with a knife, about 15 minutes. Remove the potatoes from the pot, pour out the water, and wipe out the pot. Return the potatoes to the pot.

2 • While the potatoes are steaming, stir together the flour, baking powder, salt, cinnamon, nutmeg, and allspice in a small bowl. Set aside.

3 • Position a rack in the center of the oven and preheat the oven to 350°F. Butter a 9 by 13-inch baking dish with sides at least 1½ inches high.

4 • Mash the potatoes with a masher (which will leave some lumps) or put them through a food mill or a ricer (for a smoother mixture). Stir in the butter until it is melted. Add

the brown sugar and then the flour mixture, mixing until well combined. Stir in the pineapple.

5 • Scrape the mixture into the prepared baking dish. The poon can be cooled, covered, and refrigerated for up to 2 days. Allow it to come to room temperature before proceeding.

6 • Bake for 35 to 40 minutes, until the poon is heated through and the top is beginning to brown. Remove from the oven and preheat the broiler, with the rack set 5 to 6 inches from the heat source.

7 • Place the marshmallows in a single layer over the top of the casserole. Broil until lightly browned on top, but be careful: They will catch fire very quickly!

8 • Serve immediately.

Makes 10 servings

NOTE: If you are cooking this with the turkey—which roasts at 325°F—increase the cooking time of the poon by about 15 minutes. Broil the marshmallows at the last minute, while the turkey is resting and after you've made the gravy.

TO SOFTEN 1 STICK OF BUTTER: Let the butter sit at room temperature for about 1 hour, or unwrap the butter, place it on a microwave-safe plate, and microwave at 40 percent power for 20 seconds. If not softened, continue to microwave, checking at 5-second intervals. (The time will vary slightly depending on the size and power of your microwave oven.) If you are softening less than a stick of butter, check after 5 seconds in the microwave.

Make-Ahead Mashed Potatoes

Everyone loves mashed potatoes, but I used to be the odd man out. Other than using them to build lakes and rivers with the attendant gravy, I had no use for mashed potatoes. Then I discovered Yukon Gold potatoes. Their yellowish color and creamy texture make for great mashed spuds. Consider this a mash note to mashed potatoes.

3 pounds potatoes, preferably Yukon gold (about 8 medium) or russets (about 5 medium), peeled and cut into 1-inch chunks
8 tablespoons (1 stick) unsalted butter, softened (page 25), plus more if needed

About 1 cup whole milk
Salt
Freshly ground pepper
Snipped chives or chopped parsley leaves, for serving, optional

1 • Pour 2 to 3 inches of water into a large pot and bring the water to a boil. Set the potatoes in a steamer basket over the boiling water, taking care not to let the potatoes sit in the water. Cover and steam until they can be easily pierced with a knife, about 15 minutes. Remove the potatoes from the pot, pour out the water, and wipe out the pot. Return the potatoes to the pot.

2 • Mash the potatoes with a masher (which will leave some lumps) or put them through a food mill or a ricer (for smoother potatoes). Add the butter and stir until it is melted and well combined. The potatoes can be cooled, covered, and refrigerated for up to 1 day. Allow to come to room temperature before proceeding.

3 • Pour the milk into a small saucepan over medium-high heat and cook until bubbles begin to form around the edges; do not boil. Set the pot of mashed potatoes over low heat and slowly stir in the milk until well incorporated. Season with salt and pepper. Continue heating and stirring until the potatoes are hot throughout. You can keep the potatoes hot for up to an hour before serving by placing them in the top of a double boiler or in a covered heatproof bowl set over a pot of simmering water.

4 • Sprinkle the potatoes with the chives, if desired, before serving.

Makes 8 servings

Garlic Mashed Potatoes

Cut about ½ inch off the top of 1 or 2 large heads of garlic to expose the tops of the cloves. Generously rub olive oil all over the garlic and wrap tightly in aluminum foil. Bake in a preheated 325°F oven for about 1 hour, or until the garlic can be easily pierced with a small knife. Remove from the oven and, when cool enough to handle, separate the cloves and squeeze the garlic out of the papery shell into the potatoes just before mashing. Alternatively, the roasted garlic can be cooled, covered, and refrigerated for up to 2 days.

Herbed Mashed Potatoes

Stir ⅓ cup finely chopped fresh herbs—such as thyme, rosemary, parsley, and sage into the potatoes with the milk.

Cheese Mashed Potatoes

Add 4 ounces (1 cup) crumbled, room-temperature blue cheese or grated cheddar cheese to the potatoes with the milk.

Horseradish Mashed Potatoes

Drain ¼ cup bottled grated white horseradish and add to the potatoes with the milk.

Baking Powder Biscuits

There is something inviting about a basket full of freshly baked biscuits. Now I know you can buy those premade, roll biscuits at the grocery store, but they don't taste real. A baking powder biscuit, with it's golden brown top and slight dusting of flour is the perfect accompaniment to a winter holiday meal. And as you'll see below, you can make them ahead of time.

3 cups all-purpose flour
1½ tablespoons baking powder
1½ teaspoons salt
1½ teaspoons sugar

9 tablespoons (1 stick plus 1 tablespoon) unsalted butter, chilled and cut into chunks
¾ cup whole milk, plus more if needed

1 • Position 2 racks an equal distance apart in the oven. Preheat the oven to 425°F. Lightly butter 2 baking sheets, or line them with parchment paper.

2 • Using an electric mixer or mixing by hand, combine the flour, baking powder, salt, and sugar. With the mixer, a pastry blender, or 2 knives, cut the butter into the dry ingredients until the mixture resembles coarse meal. Add the milk, stirring just until combined.

3 • Turn the dough out onto a lightly floured work surface and knead for 2 to 3 minutes until smooth and slightly elastic. Pat or gently roll out the dough ½ inch thick. Cut with a 2-inch biscuit cutter or the floured rim of a small drinking glass. Gather any scraps and pat or roll them out and cut them into rounds as well. Place the biscuits on the prepared baking sheets about 1 inch apart.

4 • Bake the biscuits for 10 to 12 minutes, switching positions of the baking sheets in the oven halfway through, until just light golden in color.

5 • Remove from the oven and let cool slightly before serving.

6 • Biscuits are best served shortly after they are made, but they can be cooled, wrapped well, and frozen for up to 1 month. Thaw and then reheat—wrapped in aluminum foil—in a preheated 450°F oven for 3 to 5 minutes.

Makes 18 to 20 biscuits

VARIATIONS

Cheese Biscuits

Add 4 ounces (1 cup) grated cheddar or Monterey Jack cheese to the biscuit dough just before you add the milk.

Herb Biscuits

Add ½ cup chopped fresh herbs (parsley, chives, or thyme) to the biscuit dough just before you add the milk.

Green Beans with Walnuts

Fresh green beans are best here, but in a pinch frozen are better than nothing. And the nuts make this vegetable somewhat more palatable to the kids at the table.

2 pounds green beans, trimmed
1 clove garlic, peeled and halved
4 tablespoons (½ stick) unsalted
   butter

1 cup finely chopped walnuts
Salt
Freshly ground pepper
2 teaspoons lemon juice, optional

1 • Fill a pot with salted water and bring to a boil. Add the beans and the garlic, reduce the heat, and simmer the beans until just tender, 10 to 15 minutes, depending on the size of the beans.

2 • Meanwhile, melt the butter in a large skillet over medium heat. Add the walnuts and cook until they begin to brown and become fragrant, 3 to 5 minutes.

3 • Drain the beans and garlic, add to the skillet, and toss until well coated; discard the garlic. Season with salt and pepper.

4 • Transfer the beans to a warm serving bowl, sprinkle with the lemon juice, if desired, and serve immediately.

Makes 8 servings

VARIATION

Green Beans with Almonds

Substitute 1 cup sliced almonds for the walnuts.

Warm Cabbage with Bacon and Apple Cider

This is a wonderful cold-weather holiday dish. Well, hopefully it's not too cold out so your guests can keep the windows rolled down on the car trip home.

---

8 strips bacon, diced
2 medium onions, peeled and cut into
    ½-inch pieces
1 medium head red cabbage (about
    2 pounds), cored and shredded,
    or 3 (10-ounce) bags shredded
    cabbage

1 cup pure maple syrup
1 cup apple cider
2 bay leaves
Salt
Freshly ground pepper

---

1 • Cook the bacon in a large heavy pot over medium-high heat, stirring, until much of the fat is rendered and the bacon begins to turn crisp and brown. Add the onions and cook, stirring, until softened, about 5 minutes. Add the cabbage and stir to combine. Add the maple syrup, cider, and bay leaves; season with salt and pepper; and stir well. Partially cover and cook over medium-low heat for 50 minutes, until the cabbage is very soft. Remove the bay leaves. The cabbage can be cooled, covered, and refrigerated for up to 24 hours. Reheat in a covered pot set over medium-low heat until the liquid begins to boil.

2 • To serve, transfer the hot cabbage to a warm serving bowl. Serve with a slotted spoon.

Makes 8 servings

Roast Acorn Squash

A side dish just doesn't get any easier than this. Roasting brings out the natural sweetness of the squash.

4 acorn squash, stemmed	*Freshly ground pepper*
Salt	*Seasoning of your choice (pages 33–34)*

1 • Position a rack in the center of the oven and preheat the oven to 375°F. Cut the squash in half lengthwise. Slice a tiny piece of skin off the bottom of each squash half so they sit level on a flat surface. Scoop out the seeds and discard them or roast them (see page 34).

2 • Place the squash halves cut side up in a large baking dish with sides at least 1½ inches high. Sprinkle the hollow of each squash lightly with salt and pepper and season as desired. If not baking immediately, cover and refrigerate for up to 24 hours.

3 • Pour hot water into the pan around the squash halves, to a depth of 1 inch (this helps keep the bottoms from burning). Cover the entire dish with aluminum foil. Bake for 45 minutes, until the flesh can just be pierced with a knife. Remove the foil and bake for an additional 15 to 20 minutes, until the flesh is very tender and beginning to brown.

4 • Serve hot.

Makes 8 servings

NOTE: If you want to put the squash in the oven with the turkey, bake it at the same temperature (325°F) but extend the cooking time to 1½ hours. Or, if you don't have enough room in your oven, you can bake the squash at 375°F, as directed, for 45 minutes. Remove the dish from the oven and let it sit, covered, at room temperature for several hours while the turkey roasts. Then, while the turkey is resting, uncover the pan and pop the squash in at 375°F for about 20 minutes, or until heated through and beginning to brown.

SUGGESTED SEASONINGS

Sweet and Cinnamon-y Squash

½ cup sweetened condensed milk ½ teaspoon ground cinnamon	4 tablespoons (½ stick) unsalted butter, cut into 8 equal pieces

In a small bowl, mix together the condensed milk and cinnamon. Spoon 1 tablespoon of the mixture into the hollow of each squash half and top each with a piece of butter.

Orange Squash

½ cup orange marmalade	4 tablespoons (½ stick) unsalted butter, cut into 8 equal pieces

Spoon 1 tablespoon marmalade into the hollow of each squash half and top with a piece of butter.

BBQ Squash

2 teaspoons chili powder ½ cup Quick Barbecue Sauce (page 205) or store-bought barbecue sauce	4 tablespoons (½ stick) unsalted butter, cut into 8 equal pieces

Sprinkle the hollow of each squash half with the chili powder. Spoon 1 tablespoon barbecue sauce into each and top with a piece of butter.

Maple-Bourbon Squash

2 teaspoons ground cinnamon	4 tablespoons (½ stick) unsalted
½ cup pure maple syrup	butter, cut into 8 equal pieces
5 tablespoons plus 1 teaspoon bourbon	

Sprinkle the hollow of each squash half with the cinnamon. Pour 1 tablespoon maple syrup and 2 teaspoons bourbon into each and top with a piece of butter.

Savory Squash

2 teaspoons ground sage	4 tablespoons (½ stick) unsalted
2 teaspoons dried thyme	butter, cut into 8 equal pieces

Sprinkle each squash half generously with the sage and thyme and top with a piece of butter.

TO ROAST SQUASH SEEDS: Separate the seeds from the stringy pulp by soaking them in a bowl of water. Dry overnight on a plate. Toss the seeds with just enough vegetable oil to coat (about 1 tablespoon will coat a cup of seeds) and sprinkle with salt. Scatter the seeds on a baking sheet and bake in a preheated 350°F oven for 35 to 45 minutes, stirring occasionally, until they begin to turn golden. Let cool completely. Store in an airtight container for up to 1 week. Use as a snack or as a garnish for squash soup (page 51) or salads.

Cranberry Sauce

You can show you care by making this fresh cranberry sauce. However, I still have not found a way to replicate the sound canned jellied cranberry sauce makes when it slurps out of the can, to lay in a quivering log on the plate.

1 cup orange juice
⅔ cup sugar
1 (12-ounce) bag fresh or thawed
*   frozen cranberries*

Salt
Freshly ground pepper

1 • Mix together the juice and sugar in a medium saucepan over medium heat. Simmer, stirring, until the sugar dissolves. Add the cranberries and cook for 10 minutes, until the berries have popped and the mixture has thickened. Season with salt and pepper and set aside to cool.

2 • Serve immediately or let cool, cover, and refrigerate for up to 4 days. Serve chilled or at room temperature.

Makes 2½ cups

Fresh Cranberry Relish

You will relish this cranberry recipe. And it's so simple, you won't get bogged down.

---

1 (12-ounce) bag fresh cranberries
1 whole orange, cut into eighths
½ small sweet onion, such as a
    Vidalia, peeled, optional

½ to 1 cup sugar
Salt
Freshly ground pepper

Combine the cranberries, unpeeled orange sections, onion, if using, and ½ cup of the sugar in a food processor. Process until finely chopped. Taste and add up to ½ cup more sugar if desired. Season with salt and pepper. Transfer the relish to a bowl and refrigerate for at least 1 day and up to 2 days before serving.

Makes 2½ cups

Pumpkin Pie with Gingersnap Crust

Forget all the other pumpkin pies you've had. This one stands out because of the gingersnap crust. Is it a snap to make? It's easy as pie. I'm sorry. I really am. I will try to restrain myself.

FOR THE CRUST (SEE NOTE)

1⅓ cups gingersnap cookie crumbs (about 25 gingersnaps)
1 tablespoon sugar
1 teaspoon ground ginger

¼ teaspoon ground cinnamon
Pinch of ground cloves
5 tablespoons unsalted butter, melted

1 • Position a rack in the center of the oven and preheat the oven to 350°F. Generously butter a 9-inch pie plate.
2 • Put the cookie crumbs in a bowl and stir in the sugar, ginger, cinnamon, and cloves. With a fork, stir in the melted butter until well mixed. Press the mixture into the prepared pie plate.
3 • Bake the pie crust for 6 minutes, until it just begins to puff up. Remove from the oven and place on a wire rack to cool. The crust can be covered with aluminum foil and stored at room temperature for up to 3 days.

FOR THE FILLING

1 (15-ounce) can pumpkin puree or 1½ cups pureed, roasted butternut squash (page 51)
2 large eggs
½ cup sugar
½ cup packed light brown sugar

¾ cup half-and-half
1 teaspoon pure vanilla extract
2 teaspoons ground ginger
1 teaspoon ground cinnamon
¼ teaspoon ground cloves
¼ teaspoon salt

1 • In a large bowl, mix together the pumpkin puree and eggs. Add the sugar, brown sugar, half-and-half, and vanilla and mix well. Stir in the ginger, cinnamon, cloves, and salt. If not baking immediately, cover and refrigerate for up to 24 hours.

2 • Position a rack in the center of the oven and preheat the oven to 350°F.

3 • Pour the filling into the crust. Bend thin strips of aluminum foil over the exposed crust on the edge of the pie plate to prevent overbrowning.

4 • Bake the pie for about 1 hour and 15 minutes, or until the center is set. It will still be jiggly, like gelatin, but the top will have colored slightly and a knife inserted in the center will come out clean. Remove the pie from the oven, discard the foil strips, and place the pie on a wire rack to cool at least partially. The pie can be cooled, covered, and refrigerated for up to 1 day or frozen, well-wrapped, for up to 1 month. (See page 39 for tips on freezing and reheating.)

5 • To serve, slice into 8 wedges and serve warm or at room temperature, with whipped cream, if desired.

Makes one 9-inch pie, or 8 servings

NOTE: You can substitute an unbaked, store-bought, single (9-inch) pie crust for the gingersnap crust. Fit the pastry into a 9-inch pie plate, cover with foil, and place dried beans, rice, or pie weights on top of the foil to keep the pie crust from puffing up. Partially bake in a preheated 425°F oven for 10 to 12 minutes, until firm but still pale. Remove the weights and the foil and let cool completely. Fill and bake the pie as directed.

How to Freeze Pies

A little advance planning goes a long way in making the holidays a breeze. Get your baking done ahead of time and you'll have more time to spend with your family on the big day. Most unbaked fruit pies and tarts, including Pear Tart with Cranberries and Almonds (page 46), freeze perfectly, well wrapped, for a month, and there's no need to defrost before baking; simply add a few minutes to the baking time. On the other hand, if you're looking to freeze Pumpkin Pie (pages 37–38) or Chocolate Pecan Pie (pages 40–41), bake them first, let cool completely, then wrap and freeze for up to a month (if a pie stays in the freezer longer than a month, it will start to deteriorate.) To thaw a frozen baked pie, unwrap and heat at 325°F for 45 minutes, or until the center is warm. Ice cream pies, such as Mud Pie (pages 154–55) also keep well in the freezer, but custard pies, including Banana Cream Pie (pages 213-14) and Sour Cream Apple Pie (pages 44–45), should never be frozen (although the unbaked crust for Sour Cream Apple Pie can be; see page 44).

Chocolate Pecan Pie

My wife, Deborah, is from the South. Each year, her mother, Ruth Roberts, sends us a sack of pecans from the pecan tree in her backyard. Here is a recipe we make to deal with this welcome annual gift. Now, if only they'd plant a cacao tree.

FOR THE CRUST

1 unbaked, store-bought, single (9-inch) pie crust
or
3/4 cup pecans
3/4 cup all-purpose flour
1/3 cup sugar

3 tablespoons unsweetened cocoa powder
1/4 teaspoon salt
1 teaspoon pure vanilla extract
6 tablespoons unsalted butter, softened (page 25)

1 • If using a store-bought crust, preheat the oven to 425°F. Fit the pastry into a 9-inch pie plate, cover with foil, and place dried beans, rice, or pie weights on top of the foil to keep the pie from puffing up. Partially bake the crust for 10 to 12 minutes, until firm but still pale. Remove the weights and the foil and let cool slightly before filling.

2 • If making the crust from scratch, position a rack in the center of the oven and preheat the oven to 375°F. Generously butter a 9-inch pie plate.

3 • Finely chop the pecans in a food processor or a clean coffee grinder, making sure to stop before they become "pecan butter." *If using a food processor,* pulse the nuts, flour, sugar, cocoa powder, and salt to blend. Add the vanilla and pulse. Then add the butter, 1 tablespoon at a time, and pulse just until a dough forms. *If mixing by hand,* stir together the nuts, flour, sugar, cocoa powder, and salt in a large bowl. Stir in the vanilla, then cut in the butter with a pastry blender or 2 knives, mixing until a dough forms. The dough can be wrapped in plastic wrap and refrigerated for up to 2 days or frozen for up to 1 month; before using, let sit at room temperature until pliable.

4 • Press the dough into the prepared pie plate. Cover the crust loosely with aluminum foil (if you cover it tightly, the foil will stick to the crust) and bake for 5 minutes. Remove the foil and bake for another 5 minutes, until the crust looks a bit dry and is beginning to puff up. Remove from the oven and let cool slightly. The crust should still be warm when you pour in the filling, as this helps it bake more evenly.

FOR THE FILLING

4 large eggs
½ cup light corn syrup
3 tablespoons unsalted butter, melted
1 tablespoon unsulphured molasses
2 teaspoons pure vanilla extract
½ cup sugar
½ cup packed light brown sugar

¼ teaspoon salt
2 ounces semisweet chocolate, finely chopped, or ⅔ cup semisweet chocolate chips, melted (page 42)
1½ cups chopped pecans, toasted (page 23)

In a large bowl, beat the eggs lightly. Add the corn syrup, butter, molasses, and vanilla and mix well. Stir in the sugar, brown sugar, and salt, then stir in the melted chocolate and mix well until thoroughly combined. Toss in the chopped pecans and stir until well distributed.

TO BAKE

1 large egg yolk, lightly beaten

1 • Position a rack in the center of the oven and preheat the oven to 375°F.
2 • Using a pastry brush, lightly coat the partially baked crust with the beaten egg yolk. Scrape the filling into the crust. Bend thin strips of aluminum foil over the exposed crust on the edge of the pie plate to prevent overbrowning.
3 • Bake the pie for 35 to 40 minutes, until the filling is just set. The edges should start to look dry and cracked, but the center will still be a bit jiggly, like gelatin, and a knife inserted in the center will come out clean. Remove the pie from the oven, discard the

foil strips, and place the pie on a wire rack to cool at least partially. The pie can be cooled, covered, and refrigerated for up to 1 day or frozen, well wrapped, for up to 1 month. (See page 39 for tips on freezing and reheating.)

4 • To serve, slice into 8 wedges and serve warm or at room temperature, with whipped cream or ice cream, if desired.

Makes one 9-inch pie, or 8 servings

TO MELT CHOCOLATE: The safest way to melt chocolate to be sure it doesn't burn is to finely chop it (if not using chocolate chips), place it in the top of a double boiler set over simmering water, and stir until melted. You can also place it in a small pot set directly over very low heat, stirring constantly, until melted. To melt chocolate in the microwave, place it in a microwave-safe container and melt on high power for 1½ minutes, then stir. Return to the microwave for 30-second intervals—stirring after each interval—until the chocolate is just melted. (The time will vary depending on the size and power of your microwave oven and how much chocolate you are melting.)

Freezing Unbaked Pie Crusts

Sweet or short dough pie crusts, like the one in the recipe for Sour Cream Apple Pie (page 44–45), can stay in the freezer, unbaked, for up to six months. Follow the recipe through placing the dough in the pan and crimping the edge. Wrap the pan in foil then cover with a large plastic bag. Seal the bag, and store in the freezer. (If you don't want your pan tied up in the freezer, use disposable, aluminum pie tins available in most grocery stores. Or after you freeze the crust, gently pry it from the pan, rewrap and return to freezer; just remember to return it to the pan when ready to fill and bake.) You do not need to thaw the crust before baking; simply add a few minutes to the oven time.

Sour Cream Apple Pie

Apple pie is about as American as . . . well, apple pie. You can trot this recipe out again during the summer holidays as well. Just add ice cream and sparklers.

FOR THE CRUST

1 unbaked, store-bought, single (9-inch) pie crust
or
1⅓ cups all-purpose flour
2 teaspoons confectioners' sugar

¼ teaspoon salt
6 tablespoons (¾ stick) unsalted butter, chilled
3 to 4 tablespoons ice water

1 • If using a store-bought crust, keep refrigerated until needed.
2 • If making the pie crust from scratch, combine the flour, sugar, and salt in a food processor or a large bowl. *If using a food processor,* add the butter and pulse until the mixture forms pea-size crumbs. *If mixing by hand,* cut in the butter with a pastry cutter or 2 knives. Add 3 tablespoons of the water and pulse or mix just until a dough forms with no crumbs in the bottom of the food processor or the bowl. If you need more water to make the dough come together, add the last tablespoon, 1 teaspoon at a time, so that you put in just what you need. Do not overmix. Gather the dough into a ball, wrap it in plastic wrap, and refrigerate for at least 1 hour or overnight. The dough can also be frozen, well wrapped, for up to 1 month; thaw before proceeding.

FOR THE TOPPING

¾ cup packed light brown sugar
8 tablespoons (1 stick) unsalted butter, softened (page 25)

1 cup chopped walnuts, pecans, or almonds
½ teaspoon ground cinnamon
⅛ teaspoon salt

In a medium bowl, mix together the brown sugar and butter to form a crumbly paste. Add the nuts, cinnamon, and salt and mix again to distribute evenly. The topping can be kept, covered, at room temperature, for up to 6 hours, or refrigerated for up to 2 days (return to room temperature before proceeding).

FOR THE FILLING

4 large Granny Smith apples (2 pounds), peeled, cored, halved, and thinly sliced	*¼ teaspoon ground cloves*
	2 large eggs
	1 cup sour cream
2 tablespoons lemon juice (from 1 lemon)	*3 tablespoons all-purpose flour*
1 cup sugar	*1 tablespoon pure vanilla extract*
1 tablespoon ground cinnamon	*¼ teaspoon salt*

1 • In a large bowl, toss the apples with the lemon juice. Add ½ cup of the sugar, the cinnamon, and the cloves and toss to coat the apples well. Set aside.

2 • In another bowl, beat together the remaining ½ cup sugar, eggs, sour cream, flour, vanilla, and salt until smooth.

3 • Position a rack in the center of the oven and preheat the oven to 400°F.

4 • Turn out the dough onto a lightly floured work surface and, using a lightly floured rolling pin, roll out the dough to fit a 9-inch pie plate. Keep moving and flouring the dough as you roll so that it does not stick to the work surface. Transfer the dough carefully to the pie plate, pressing the dough into the pie plate and patching any tears. Trim any excess dough to ½ inch of the edge, fold the extra dough under, and use your fingers or a fork to crimp decoratively.

5 • Layer the apples in the crust, pouring any juices that have accumulated in the bowl over the apples. Pour the sour cream mixture over the apples. Using your hands, crumble the topping evenly over the pie.

6 • Bake the pie for 10 minutes. Reduce the oven temperature to 350°F and bake for 35 to 40 minutes, until the topping is quite brown and bubbling. Remove the pie from the oven and place on a wire rack to cool slightly.

7 • Serve the pie warm or at room temperature. This pie is best eaten the day it is made.

Makes one 9-inch pie, or 8 servings

Pear Tart with Cranberries and Almonds

I really enjoy pears. A fresh crisp pear or a slightly soft, sweet one makes a great dessert by itself. Here's a way to improve on it.

1 (10 by 10-inch square) sheet frozen puff pastry (half of a 17.3-ounce package), thawed according to package directions
2 tablespoons sugar

2 Bosc, Anjou, or other pears (½ pound), stemmed, halved, and cored
¼ cup dried cranberries or dried cherries
¼ cup sliced almonds
2 tablespoons unsalted butter, melted

1 • Position a rack in the center of the oven and preheat the oven to 425°F.

2 • Place the puff pastry on a baking sheet. Sprinkle with 1 tablespoon of the sugar.

3 • Using a sharp knife, cut the pears lengthwise into ⅛-inch slices. Place the slices in neat, slightly overlapping rows on the pastry, leaving a ¾-inch border of exposed dough all around. Sprinkle the dried cranberries and almonds over the pears. Brush the top of the tart with the melted butter and sprinkle with the remaining 1 tablespoon sugar. The tart can be covered and refrigerated for up to 24 hours or frozen, well wrapped, for up to 1 month.

4 • Bake until the pears are soft and lightly colored, and the pastry is golden, about 18 minutes (1 or 2 minutes longer, if frozen). Remove from the oven and let cool for at least 10 minutes.

5 • The tart is best served warm, but it can also be served at room temperature. Serve with whipped cream or vanilla ice cream, if desired.

Makes one 10-inch square tart, or 10 servings

Christmas Dinner

Christmas is one of those holidays that encompasses a few days and involves several meals. When I was a kid, it was a big deal to be old enough to go to Midnight Mass, and that also meant I got to participate in the post–Midnight Mass meal. Relatives would bring dishes after church and then line 'em up on the dining room table and we'd eat. There was also plenty of too-rich eggnog, one bowl for the kids, another for the adults (wink-wink). After the meal, we'd exchange presents and finally hit the sack for a few hours before the younger siblings would wake up.

After there was much tearing of wrapping paper, squealing, and oooohing and aaaahing over presents, Mom would whip up a big breakfast of bacon and eggs, pancakes, and sausages. Once we were all fed, it was time to clean up and begin cooking for the big Christmas meal. I don't think the oven would be turned off for a seventy-two-hour period.

That was before we got wise to the concept of brunch. Today, it's a great way to handle the drop-in guests who stop by to give and get some holiday cheer.

Eggnog

In my youth, our family's eggnog was purchased at the store and doctored with ingredients from my Dad's liquor cabinet. It was fattening, alcoholic, and a rare adult treat we got to try once a year. Today, making from-scratch eggnog is something I enjoy doing. It's one of those times that I think your guests can tell and appreciate the difference between homemade and store-bought. Just remember, too much alcohol ruins the flavor. You do want your guests to a) remember what they had and b) be able to leave under their own power.

1 quart whole milk
8 large eggs
¾ cup sugar
Pinch of salt
1 teaspoon pure vanilla extract

2 cups heavy cream
1 to 1½ cups bourbon, brandy, or rum,
*   optional*
Ground nutmeg
Ground cinnamon

1 • Fill a large bowl halfway with ice and cold water. Set out a smaller bowl (with a minimum capacity of 2 quarts) that will fit inside the larger bowl.

2 • Warm 2 cups of the milk in a saucepan over medium heat until bubbles form around the edge. Do not boil.

3 • In a medium bowl, whisk together the eggs, sugar, and salt until well blended. Gradually whisk in the hot milk. Pour the mixture into the saucepan and cook over low heat, stirring constantly with a stainless steel or wooden spoon, until the mixture is thick enough to coat the back of the spoon. This should take 5 to 8 minutes, and the mixture should register about 165°F on an instant-read thermometer.

4 • Stir in the remaining 2 cups milk. Pour the mixture into the smaller bowl that you have set out and place this bowl in the prepared ice water bath. Stir to cool the mixture. When cool, stir in the vanilla and 1 cup of the heavy cream. Cover and refrigerate until thoroughly chilled, at least 4 hours and up to 24 hours.

5 • When ready to serve, pour the mixture into a punch bowl or other large container. Stir

in the brandy, if using. Whip the remaining 1 cup of cream and gently fold it into the eggnog. Sprinkle with nutmeg and cinnamon and serve immediately, using a ladle to spoon the eggnog into glasses or punch cups.

Makes sixteen to twenty 4-ounce servings

Store-Bought Eggnog with a Twist

Jazz up store-bought eggnog by adding any or all of the following: ground cinnamon, ground nutmeg, ground mace, whipped cream, or bourbon, brandy, or rum (or sherry).

Mulled Wine

This is always a welcome addition on a cold winter night, and the alcohol content is a little lower than some other beverages you could serve during the holidays.

1½ cups sugar
1½ cups water
Zest of 1 orange, removed in wide strips with a vegetable peeler
Zest of 1 lemon, removed in wide strips with a vegetable peeler

2 cinnamon sticks
⅔ cup orange juice (from 2 oranges)
½ cup lemon juice (from 2 to 3 lemons)
2 (1.5- liter) or 4 (750-milliliter) bottles red wine

---

1 • Combine the sugar, water, orange and lemon zests, and cinnamon sticks in a large saucepan over high heat. Bring to a boil, then lower the heat and simmer, stirring occasionally, for 5 minutes. Strain the syrup, discarding the zests and cinnamon sticks. The syrup can be cooled, covered, and refrigerated for up to 1 month.

2 • Pour the syrup, orange and lemon juices, and wine into a large pot. Cook over medium heat, stirring occasionally, until very hot; do not boil. Serve immediately, ladling the wine into mugs.

Makes thirty-two 4-ounce servings

Creamy Squash Soup

There is something decadent about a luscious, creamy squash soup that makes it perfect for fall and winter holidays.

2 butternut squash (2½ pounds each), or 3 (15-ounce) cans pumpkin puree
3 tablespoons extra-virgin olive oil
2 medium onions, peeled and finely chopped
2 tablespoons finely grated orange zest (from 2 to 3 oranges)
1½ teaspoons ground ginger
1 teaspoon ground cinnamon
Pinch of ground cloves
7 cups canned chicken broth
⅓ cup Madeira or ruby port
¾ cup heavy cream
Salt
Freshly ground pepper

1 • If using butternut squash, position a rack in the middle of the oven and preheat the oven to 350°F.

2 • Cut the squash in half lengthwise and scoop out the seeds and discard them or roast them (see page 34). Place the squash cut side down on a rimmed baking sheet. Bake for about 1 hour, until the tough skin can be easily pierced with a knife. Remove from the oven and let cool. Scrape the pulp out into a food processor or blender and pulse to puree. (A food mill or ricer will also do the trick.) You will need about 4½ cups of puree for the soup. The puree can be cooled, covered, and refrigerated for up to 4 days or frozen, well wrapped, for up to 2 months (if frozen, thaw before proceeding).

3 • Warm the oil in a pot over medium-high heat. Add the onions and cook, stirring, until softened but not browned, about 5 minutes. Add the squash puree, orange zest, ginger, cinnamon, and cloves and stir to combine. Pour in the broth and Madeira, partially cover the saucepan, and cook over medium-low heat for 15 to 20 minutes, stirring occasionally, until the soup is heated through and the flavors have blended. The soup can be cooled, covered, and refrigerated for up to 24 hours or frozen, well wrapped, for up to 1 month (if frozen, thaw and reheat before proceeding).

4 • Add the heavy cream and season with salt and pepper. Simmer, stirring occasionally, until the soup is very hot, but do not allow it to boil.

5 • Ladle into 8 warm bowls and serve.

Makes about 12 cups, or 8 servings

Fennel Salad with Orange-Mustard Vinaigrette

For those looking to maybe keep things in check, calorically, we offer this salad. Good luck.

FOR THE DRESSING

¼ cup red wine vinegar
2 tablespoons finely grated orange zest
1 teaspoon Dijon mustard

1 teaspoon salt
¼ teaspoon freshly ground pepper
½ cup extra-virgin olive oil

In a blender, combine the vinegar, orange zest, mustard, salt, and pepper. With the machine on, pour the oil in slowly, so that it is incorporated into the dressing and creates an emulsion. The dressing can be covered and refrigerated for up to 1 week.

FOR THE SALAD

3 medium bulbs fennel
1 small red onion, peeled and cut into
  ¼-inch pieces

1 red bell pepper, stemmed, seeded,
  and cut into ¼-inch pieces
Several large lettuce leaves, rinsed
  and dried

1 • Trim the stalks and the feathery fronds from the fennel, reserving a few of the fronds for garnish. Halve and core the fennel, then chop coarsely and transfer to a medium bowl. Add the onion and bell pepper and toss with enough dressing to coat the vegetables well. Cover and refrigerate for at least 1 hour and up to 6 hours.

2 • Line a serving platter with the lettuce leaves. Spoon the salad onto the leaves. Garnish with a few of the reserved fennel fronds and serve.

Makes 8 servings

Red and Green Christmas Salad

Another salad, a little more fattening. But hey, it's Christmas. You still have a few more days until you need to make New Year's resolutions.

FOR THE BLUE CHEESE DRESSING

¾ cup mayonnaise
¾ cup sour cream
4 ounces crumbled blue cheese (½ cup)
2 tablespoons lemon juice (from 1 lemon)

2 cloves garlic, peeled and finely chopped
Pinch of cayenne pepper
Salt
Freshly ground pepper

In a food processor or a blender, combine all of the ingredients, season with salt and pepper, and puree until smooth. The dressing can be covered and refrigerated for up to 2 days.

FOR THE SALAD

8 slices bacon, diced
1 head radicchio, leaves separated
   (2 to 3 cups)
10 cups lightly packed baby spinach
   (10 ounces)

10 ounces button mushrooms, wiped
   clean and sliced
1 red bell pepper, stemmed, seeded,
   and thinly sliced
¼ cup pine nuts, toasted (page 23),
   optional

1 • Line a plate with several sheets of paper towels. Cook the bacon in a skillet over medium-high heat, stirring occasionally, until crisp, about 10 minutes. Using a slotted spoon, transfer the bacon to the prepared plate to drain.
2 • Tear the radicchio leaves into bite-size pieces and toss them in a large bowl with the spinach, mushrooms, and bell pepper. Sprinkle the bacon and pine nuts, if using, on top.
3 • Just before serving, add the dressing and toss to coat the ingredients.

Makes 8 servings

Roast Beef Tenderloin with Cracked Pepper Crust and Horseradish Cream

You want at least one entrée that's going to make your guests unfasten their pants or skirts when all is said and done. This is the one. Ho Ho Ho.

FOR THE HORSERADISH CREAM

¼ cup bottled grated white horseradish, drained	Salt
	Freshly ground pepper
2 tablespoons lemon juice (from 1 lemon)	1 cup heavy cream

1 • In a small bowl, combine the horseradish and lemon juice, and season with salt and pepper.

2 • Using an electric mixer or a wire whisk, whip the cream until it holds stiff peaks. Fold the horseradish mixture into the whipped cream. Cover and refrigerate for at least 30 minutes, and up to 4 hours, for the flavors to blend.

FOR THE BEEF

1 (3½- to 4-pound) beef tenderloin	1 teaspoon coarse salt, such as kosher salt
2 cloves garlic, peeled	
3 tablespoons fresh rosemary leaves or 2 tablespoons dried rosemary	2 teaspoons finely grated orange zest (from 1 orange)
2 tablespoons whole black peppercorns	1 tablespoon extra-virgin olive oil

1 • Position a rack in the center of the oven and preheat the oven to 450°F. Lightly oil a small roasting pan fitted with a rack (oiling the pan will help keep the pan drippings from sticking).

2 • Rinse the meat under cold running water and pat it dry with paper towels. Using a small, sharp knife, cut a half dozen small slits in the meat. Cut 1 clove of garlic into slivers, and tuck the slivers into the slits.

3 • In a mini food processor, spice grinder, or clean coffee grinder, or using a mortar and pestle, grind the rosemary, peppercorns, and coarse salt together until the peppercorns are well cracked. Add the remaining clove garlic and the orange zest and grind until all of the ingredients are mashed. Slowly add the oil to form a paste.

4 • Pat the peppercorn paste all over the meat. Place the meat on the rack in the prepared pan and roast for 10 minutes. Reduce the oven temperature to 375°F and roast for an additional 40 to 45 minutes, or until a meat thermometer or an instant-read thermometer inserted in the center of the meat registers 145°F for medium-rare.

5 • Remove the pan from the oven and transfer the meat to a cutting board. Cover with a piece of aluminum foil to keep warm and let rest for at least 5 minutes before carving. Slice and serve on a warm platter, drizzled with any juices that have collected in the roasting pan or on the cutting board. Pass the horseradish cream in a small sauceboat at the table.

Makes 8 servings

Crown Pork Roast with Fruit Stuffing

Here's a crowning glory. Trust me, your guests will remember this pork roast not only because it is delicious, but because it makes a very dramatic presentation, perfect for a celebration.

FOR THE PORK

*1 (8- to 10-pound) crown pork roast,
   14 to 16 chops
2 cloves garlic, smashed and peeled*

*Coarse salt
Freshly ground pepper*

1 • Position a rack in the center of the oven and preheat the oven to 450°F. Lightly oil a large roasting pan (oiling the pan will help keep the meat and the pan drippings from sticking).

2 • Separate the chops with your fingers and rub the surfaces of the meat in between the chops with the garlic, discarding the garlic when you are done. Sprinkle the meat with coarse salt and pepper and cover the exposed bones with small pieces of aluminum foil to keep them from burning. Transfer the roast to the prepared pan, place the pan in the oven, and immediately reduce the heat to 325°F. The roast will need to cook for about 20 minutes per pound, or between 2 hours and 40 minutes for an 8-pound roast and 3 hours and 20 minutes for a 10-pound roast. While the meat is roasting, make the stuffing.

FOR THE STUFFING

*1 tablespoon extra-virgin olive oil
1 medium onion, peeled and cut into
   1/4-inch pieces
1 clove garlic, peeled and finely chopped
2 tablespoons peeled, finely chopped
   fresh ginger
2 tablespoons finely grated orange
   zest (from 2 to 3 oranges)
1 cup chopped pitted prunes*

*1 cup chopped dried apricots
1/2 cup dried cherries or cranberries
1 cup dried bread cubes (page 21) or
   packaged stuffing or croutons
1 cup chopped walnuts, toasted
   (page 23)
1/2 cup orange juice (from 2 oranges)
Salt
Freshly ground pepper*

1 • Warm the oil in a pot over high heat. Add the onion and cook, stirring, until softened but not browned, about 5 minutes. Add the garlic, ginger, and orange zest and cook for 2 minutes more. Remove from the heat. Stir in the prunes, apricots, and cherries. Then stir in the bread, walnuts, and orange juice. Season with salt and pepper.

2 • When the roast has about an hour more to cook, remove it from the oven and fill the center cavity with as much stuffing as it will hold. Put any remaining stuffing in a small baking dish, cover with aluminum foil, and set aside for the moment.

3 • Return the pork to the oven and continue roasting. The roast is done when a meat thermometer or an instant-read thermometer inserted in the thickest part of the meat registers at least 160°F for medium.

4 • Remove the roasting pan from the oven, and carefully transfer the stuffed roast to a warm platter. Cover loosely with aluminum foil to keep warm, and let it rest for 15 minutes. Put the small baking dish of extra stuffing into the oven to bake for 15 to 20 minutes while you prepare the gravy.

FOR THE GRAVY

½ cup dry white wine
2 tablespoons all-purpose flour

½ to 1 cup canned chicken broth

1• Set the roasting pan over 2 burners and warm over low heat, stirring in the wine, and scraping up any browned bits from the bottom. Cook for 3 to 5 minutes, until the wine has reduced by about half. Add the flour and stir until smooth. Add ½ cup of the chicken broth and heat slowly, stirring occasionally, until the gravy thickens, 8 to 10 minutes. If too thick, add more chicken broth, a bit at a time, until the desired consistency is reached.

2 • Present the roast at the table and carve by cutting it into individual pork chops. Serve 1 or 2 chops per person, drizzled with a bit of gravy and topped with a spoonful of stuffing. (Remember to remove the extra dish of stuffing from the oven and bring it to the table as well.)

Makes 8 to 10 servings

Christmas Leftovers

Remember, any holiday meal is likely to have leftovers, not just Thanksgiving. These recipes make tasty use of Roast Beef Tenderloin with Cracked Pepper Crust and Horseradish Cream (pages 54–55) and Crown Pork Roast with Fruit Stuffing (pages 56–57) and will have you looking forward to leftovers.

SECOND-DAY BEEF STROGANOFF

Melt 2 tablespoons (¼ stick) unsalted butter in a medium saucepan over medium heat, add 1 finely chopped medium onion and 2 cloves minced garlic, and cook for about 5 minutes. Add 3 cups diced, leftover roast beef and cook, stirring, until hot. Stir in 2 tablespoons tomato paste, 1 cup canned beef gravy, and 1 cup sour cream and cook until just heated through. Serve over egg noodles or mashed potatoes. Makes 4 servings.

HASH

Cut 4 medium Yukon gold potatoes into ½-inch pieces and steam until tender (page 26), about 10 minutes. Chop 2 or 3 slices of bacon and cook in a skillet over medium-high heat until almost crisp. Add 1 chopped medium onion and cook, stirring, until softened but not browned, about 5 minutes. Add the potato. Add 2 cups of leftover roast beef or pork cut into ½-inch cubes, season with salt and pepper, and continue cooking, without turning, until a crust begins to form on the bottom. Turn the hash over in sections and cook until well browned on the other side. Serve with fried or poached eggs and toast. Makes 4 servings.

BEANS AND RICE WITH PORK

Cook 1 cup white or brown rice according to package directions. Meanwhile, warm 2 tablespoons olive oil in a large saucepan over medium heat; add 2 cloves garlic,

1 chopped medium onion, and 1 chopped red or green bell pepper and cook for about 10 minutes. Mix the rice together with the vegetables and one 15½-ounce can of black beans or red kidney beans (drained and rinsed), and 2 cups cooked pork, cut into ½-inch pieces. If desired, add one 4-ounce jar pimientos, drained. Heat through and serve with hot sauce on the side. Makes 4 servings.

CUBAN SANDWICH

Make a sandwich on a submarine-shaped loaf of Cuban, French, or Italian bread. Layer it with mustard, mayonnaise, sliced pork, ham, Swiss cheese, tomato, and dill pickle. Coat the outside of the bread with butter and put it in a skillet over medium heat. Weight the sandwich as you cook it by pressing firmly with a spatula or placing another skillet on top. Flip and give the other side equal treatment until the bread is crisp. Serve immediately.

Braised Endive with Orange Zest

I know Mom always told you to eat your veggies. If my Mom made veggies like this more often, I wouldn't have had to have been told so much.

6 medium Belgian endive (about
    1½ pounds)
2 tablespoons unsalted butter
1 shallot, peeled and finely chopped
2 teaspoons finely grated orange zest
    (from 1 orange)

¼ cup orange juice (from 1 orange)
¼ cup dry white wine
Salt
Freshly ground pepper

1 • Pull off any split or browned or otherwise damaged outer leaves of the endive. Trim the pointed end only if it is discolored. Run each endive briefly under cold running water; pat dry. Cut each endive in half lengthwise—the stem will hold the leaves together.

2 • Melt the butter in a large, preferably nonstick, skillet over medium heat until it begins to foam. Add the endive halves and brown lightly, turning as needed, about 5 minutes. Add the shallot, orange zest, orange juice, and wine. Season with salt and pepper, turn the heat to low, and simmer for about 45 minutes, or until the endive is very tender. The endive can be cooled, covered, and refrigerated for up to 24 hours. Reheat gently before serving.

3 • Serve the endive fanned out on a warm platter and drizzle with the pan juices.

Makes 6 servings

Sautéed Kale

Kale is one of those greens that my wife grew up with in the South. It's usually cooked with a big ol' piece of salt pork or fatback thrown in for good measure. This version uses olive oil and a little spice. Kale, Kale, the gang's all here!

2½ pounds kale
6 tablespoons extra-virgin olive oil
3 large cloves garlic, peeled and
*   coarsely chopped*

½ teaspoon hot red pepper flakes
Salt
Freshly ground pepper
Cider vinegar

---

1 • Remove the tough stems and center ribs from the kale. Tear or chop the leaves into bite-size pieces. Rinse the kale well and put it in a bowl of cold water.

2 • Warm the olive oil in a large pot over medium-high heat. Add the garlic and red pepper flakes, and cook, stirring, for 3 to 5 minutes. Drain the kale quickly in a colander, leaving some water on the leaves. Put it in the pot and season with salt and pepper. Cook, stirring, for 5 minutes, then lower the heat to medium-low and cook, stirring occasionally, until the kale is tender, 15 to 20 minutes. The kale can be cooled, covered, and refrigerated for up to 24 hours. Reheat gently before serving.

3 • To serve, spoon the kale and any juices from the pot into a warm serving bowl and finish with a splash of cider vinegar.

Makes 8 servings

Scalloped Potatoes

Scalloped potatoes usually came out of a box in our house when I was a kid. These amazing scalloped potatoes make me forget that early childhood trauma.

3 pounds Yukon gold or other yellow
   potatoes (about 8 medium)
1 large onion, peeled and sliced
   crosswise into thin rings
6 tablespoons (¾ stick) unsalted
   butter, cut into small pieces

Salt
Freshly ground pepper
2 cups heavy cream
1 cup whole milk

1 • Position a rack in the center of the oven and preheat the oven to 325°F. Lightly butter a 9 by 13-inch baking dish with sides at least 1½ inches high.

2 • Peel the potatoes and slice them thinly—you can do this with a sharp knife, a mandoline, or a food processor fitted with a slicing blade. Place one-third of the potatoes in an even layer in the prepared dish. Scatter half of the onion rings on top, dot with 2 tablespoons of the butter, and sprinkle generously with salt and pepper. Repeat to make a second layer, and top with a final layer of potatoes. Season with salt and pepper. Pour the cream and milk into the dish.

3 • Bake, uncovered, for 1½ hours, or until the potatoes are extremely tender when pierced with a knife, and the top is lightly browned. The potatoes can be cooled, covered, and refrigerated for up to 24 hours. Bring to room temperature and reheat, covered, in a preheated 325°F oven for about 20 minutes.

4 • Serve from the baking dish, scooping up any creamy liquid with the potatoes.

Makes 8 servings

Spoon Bread

Because of Deborah, I find myself an honorary Southerner. Actually I am a little jealous of her culinary heritage. We had more of a Caribbean-American generic cuisine going on in our house. So I have enjoyed learning to cook some of the dishes I'm served when we're down there visiting her family. This is one of them.

1 cup water	1 cup cornmeal
2 cups whole milk	3 tablespoons unsalted butter, chilled
1 teaspoon salt	3 large eggs

1 • Position a rack in the center of the oven and preheat the oven to 375°F. Lightly butter a 3-quart baking dish.

2 • Bring the water and 1 cup of the milk to a boil in a medium pot. Add the salt and slowly stir in the cornmeal. Reduce the heat and simmer, stirring, until the mixture begins to thicken, about 2 minutes. Remove from the heat and stir in the butter. Let cool slightly, stirring vigorously for a few strokes to let heat escape.

3 • *For dense, custardy spoon bread*: Whisk together the eggs and the remaining cup milk and stir them into the cornmeal mixture. Pour into the prepared baking dish. This version can be cooled, covered, and refrigerated for up to 24 hours before baking.

4 • *For lighter, soufflé-like spoon bread*: Separate the eggs. Whisk together the yolks with the remaining cup milk and stir into the cornmeal mixture. In a large, very clean bowl (any trace of grease will keep the whites from whipping to their fullest volume), whip the egg whites with an electric mixer on high speed until they hold stiff peaks, and then gently fold them into the cornmeal mixture with a spatula. Pour into the prepared baking dish, lightly smoothing the top.

5 • Bake the spoon bread for 35 to 40 minutes, or until a table knife inserted in the center comes out clean.

6 • Serve hot from the baking dish.

Makes 8 servings

Red Velvet Cake

Born and raised in Perry, Georgia, Deborah likes her desserts. To look at her, you'd never know it, but she can throw down a dessert or two. A couple of years ago, we were going over our Christmas dinner menu and Deborah said, "I'd really love a Red Velvet Cake."

"What the heck is that?" I asked. Deborah patiently explained to her Yankee husband that Red Velvet Cake is a chocolate cake, colored red, with rich icing. At that, my ears perked up. See, I look at frosted layer cake as two desserts. I eat the cake first and leave the frosting for the final dessert. But where the heck was I going to get a Red Velvet Cake?

I turned to our good friend Spenser Means, a premier real estate agent in New York City and a good-looking African American gentleman who knows how and where to get anything. I called Spenser, and before I could finish describing it, Spenser said, "I will bring the cake. What time is dinner?"

Spenser arrived with a 14-inch cake with white frosting sprinkled with crushed walnuts from a great bakery in Harlem called Make My Cake. It made our night because the cake was so wonderfully smooth inside it was, well, velvety, and the icing was so rich it could stand on its own.

Here's your opportunity to make your own Red Velvet memory.

FOR THE CAKE

½ cup solid vegetable shortening
2 cups sugar
3 large eggs
1 teaspoon pure vanilla extract
2¼ cups all-purpose flour
½ cup unsweetened cocoa powder

1 teaspoon baking soda
1 teaspoon salt
1 cup buttermilk
1 tablespoon cider vinegar
1 to 4 tablespoons red food coloring

1 • Position a rack in the center of the oven and preheat the oven to 350°F.

2 • Butter two 9-inch cake pans and dust with flour.

3 • Using an electric mixer or mixing by hand, beat together the shortening and sugar until fluffy, at least 3 minutes. Add the eggs, one at a time, beating well after each addition. Beat in the vanilla.

4 • In a small bowl, stir together the flour, cocoa powder, baking soda, and salt. In another bowl, combine the buttermilk, vinegar, and food coloring (1 tablespoon will give you a dark brown-red, the color will become brighter the more food coloring you add). Gradually stir the dry ingredients into the egg mixture, alternating with the buttermilk mixture, until all ingredients are just incorporated and the batter is smooth. Do not overmix. Using a rubber spatula, scrape the batter evenly into the 2 prepared pans.

5 • Bake for about 35 minutes, until the cake just begins to pull away from the sides of the pans and a knife inserted in the center of each comes out clean.

6 • Remove from the oven, place on wire racks, and let cool for about 15 minutes. Run a knife around the edge of the pans, and remove the cakes from the pans by inverting them onto the racks. Turn right side up and let cool thoroughly. The cakes can be stored, well wrapped, at room temperature for up to 2 days or frozen for up to 2 months. If frozen, thaw at room temperature before proceeding.

FOR THE FROSTING

3 tablespoons all-purpose flour	*16 tablespoons (2 sticks) unsalted butter, softened (page 25)*
Pinch of salt	*1 cup sugar*
1 cup whole milk	*1 tablespoon pure vanilla extract*

1 • In a small saucepan combine the flour, salt, and a few tablespoons of the milk, stirring until smooth. Set the saucepan over low heat and stir in the remaining milk. Cook, stirring, until the mixture thickens to the consistency of gravy, about 5 minutes. Remove from the heat and let cool to room temperature.

2 • Using an electric mixer, beat together the butter, sugar, and vanilla for a minute or so until smooth. Scrape the cooled flour mixture into the butter mixture and beat on high speed for about 3 minutes, until the frosting is the consistency of whipped cream. The frosting can be covered and refrigerated for up to 2 days; let sit at room temperature for about 15 minutes to reach a spreadable consistency.

3 • Place 1 layer of the cake on a serving plate and spread with a little less than half the frosting. Place the remaining cake layer on top and frost the top and sides with the remaining frosting.

4 • The cake can be stored, loosely covered, at room temperature for up to 24 hours or frozen, well wrapped, for up to 1 month. If frozen, let the cake come to room temperature before serving.

Makes one 9-inch layer cake, or about 10 servings

NOTE: If you want to store a cake at room temperature and you don't have a cake cover, store it under a large, inverted mixing bowl or the bottom of a salad spinner.

Christmas Brunch

The presents have been opened, everyone's showered and dressed. It's time to eat, but it's a little late to eat breakfast. What to have? Time for Christmas Brunch. We started this tradition recently and it's a lot of fun. Breakfast coexisting with lunch on a festive day cuts the hassle quotient in half and gives you the chance to be a little creative.

Citrus Salad with Raspberry-Lime Puree

Here's a light, refreshing, great start for a brunch. Given that last night's eggnog is still weighing you down, this is the way to go.

½ cup sugar
½ cup water
Zest of 1 lime, removed in wide strips
    with a vegetable peeler
1 (12-ounce) package frozen
    raspberries (3 cups)
1 tablespoon lime juice (from 1 lime)
4 navel oranges

3 small pink grapefruits
½ fresh pineapple, peeled, cored, and
    cut into 1-inch chunks (2 cups)
½ cup chopped crystallized ginger
    (available in supermarkets),
    optional
Fresh mint, for serving, optional

1 • Combine the sugar, water, and lime zest in a small saucepan. Bring to a boil, and then lower the heat and simmer, stirring occasionally, for 5 minutes. Remove from the heat and let cool to room temperature. Strain the syrup, discarding the zest. The syrup can be covered and refrigerated for up to 1 month.

2 • Combine the sugar syrup with 2 cups of the raspberries and the lime juice in a blender. Puree until smooth. The puree can be covered and refrigerated for up to 3 days.

3 • Set the oranges and grapefruits on a cutting board and, using a sharp knife, peel each fruit, slicing away the bitter white pith along with a thin sliver of flesh. Slice between the membranes of each fruit to cut into sections. Cut each section in half. Put the fruit in a serving bowl, squeeze the juice from the membranes on top before discarding, and add the pineapple, the remaining cup of raspberries, and the ginger, if using. Toss to combine. The salad can be covered and refrigerated for up to 12 hours.

4 • Just before serving, toss the salad with the raspberry puree and garnish with fresh mint, if desired.

Makes 10 servings

Breakfast Strata

Is it a lunch dish, a breakfast dish, or both? Depends on what time of day you set it out. All I know is, it's good and you can make it up ahead of time.

4 cups homemade croutons (see below) or 1 (6-ounce) box store-bought croutons, plain or seasoned

8 ounces grated cheddar or Monterey Jack cheese (2 cups)

8 large eggs

1 quart whole milk

1 teaspoon Dijon mustard or dried dill, optional

Salt

Freshly ground pepper

1 • Position a rack in the center of the oven and preheat the oven to 350°F. Lightly butter a 4-quart baking dish.

2 • Combine the croutons and cheese in the prepared baking dish. In a bowl, whisk together the eggs, milk, and mustard or dill, if using, and season with salt and pepper. Pour this mixture over the croutons and cheese. The mixture can be covered and refrigerated for up to 24 hours.

3 • Bake for 50 to 60 minutes, until puffed, golden, and set in the center. Remove from the oven and let cool slightly. Serve from the baking dish.

Makes 10 servings

TO MAKE 4 CUPS CROUTONS: Cut half of a 1-pound loaf of bread (preferably French or Italian, but white, whole wheat, or multigrain bread will work) into ½-inch cubes and scatter them on a rimmed baking sheet. Drizzle lightly with 2 tablespoons olive oil and season with salt and pepper, as well as with 1 teaspoon of any of the following, if desired: garlic powder, onion powder, dried basil, or dried oregano. Bake in a preheated 375°F oven for 10 to 15 minutes, stirring once or twice, until browned and crisp. Remove from the pan and let cool. The croutons can be stored in an airtight container for up to 1 week.

Blueberry Coffee Cake

Who doesn't like coffee cake? With that streusel topping, it's like two desserts in one. Like frosting, I save my streusel topping till the end. Although with this recipe . . . it's awfully hard.

FOR THE STREUSEL

2/3 cup brown sugar
1/2 cup all-purpose flour
1 teaspoon ground cinnamon
1/4 teaspoon ground nutmeg

6 tablespoons (3/4 stick) unsalted
    butter, cut into 6 chunks
1 cup chopped walnuts or pecans,
    toasted (page 23)

1 • In a food processor or a medium bowl, mix together the brown sugar, flour, cinnamon, and nutmeg. Scatter the butter on top of the mixture. *If using a food processor,* pulse until large clumps form; transfer the mixture to a bowl. *If working by hand,* cut the butter into the flour mixture using a pastry blender or 2 knives.

2 • Break up the clumps a little with your hands. Stir in the nuts until evenly distributed. The streusel can be covered and refrigerated for up to 2 days (let come to room temperature and crumble any big clumps if needed before proceeding).

FOR THE CAKE

6 tablespoons (3/4 stick) unsalted
    butter, softened (page 25)
3/4 cup packed light brown sugar
1 large egg
1 cup sour cream
1 teaspoon pure vanilla extract

2 cups all-purpose flour
1 tablespoon baking powder
1 teaspoon salt
2 cups fresh blueberries, rinsed and
    picked over, or frozen blueberries,
    thawed

1 • Position a rack in the center of the oven and preheat the oven to 350°F.

2 • Generously butter a 9-inch springform pan.

3 • Using an electric mixer or mixing by hand, beat together the butter and brown sugar until light and fluffy, about 3 minutes. Add the egg and beat for 30 seconds longer. Mix in the sour cream and vanilla until well combined.

4 • In a small bowl, stir together the flour, baking powder, and salt. Add to the butter mixture and beat just until incorporated. Do not overmix.

5 • Spoon half the batter into the prepared pan, smoothing the top with a flat metal spatula or a butter knife. Sprinkle the blueberries over the batter, and then top with half the streusel. Spoon the remaining batter on top, and then sprinkle the remaining streusel over the top.

6 • Bake the cake for 45 to 55 minutes, or until a knife inserted in the center comes out clean. Remove from the oven and set on a wire rack to cool. When cool, run a knife around the edge of the pan and remove the sides. Serve warm or at room temperature.

7 • This cake does not freeze well, but, once cool, can be stored at room temperature, well wrapped, for up to 3 days.

Makes 10 servings

VARIATION

Apple Coffee Cake

Substitute 2 cups chopped, peeled tart apples (such as Granny Smiths) for the blueberries.

Brunch Beverages

- A pitcher of well-chilled orange juice is perfect, but see the ideas for *Festive Juice Drinks* (page 11) for something different. A combination of orange juice and chilled champagne makes a classic mimosa (page 113).

- You'll want hot coffee—and plenty of it—to accompany your brunch. Brew it as close to serving as possible to keep the flavor fresh. Have available milk, cream, and sweeteners (see below), and consider trying these variations:

- *Cinnamon Coffee:* Add a generous pinch of cinnamon to the ground coffee just before you brew it.

- *Cafe au Lait:* Set a saucepan of milk over medium-high heat and bring it almost to a boil—you will see little bubbles at the edges of the milk. Combine equal amounts of coffee and milk in large, warm mugs.

- *Cafe Mocha:* Mix together equal parts hot cocoa (below) and hot coffee, and top with Mocha Whipped Cream (below), if desired.

- Hot cocoa is always welcome on a winter morning. In a saucepan, stir together $1/4$ cup unsweetened cocoa powder, 3 tablespoons sugar, and a dash of salt with $1/2$ cup milk to make a paste. Set the pot over medium heat and, stirring constantly, slowly add $3 1/2$ cups milk. Remove from the heat when tiny bubbles appear (do not boil) and stir in $1/2$ teaspoon pure vanilla extract. Top with Cinnamon Whipped Cream (see opposite) or marshmallows, if desired. This makes four 1-cup servings.

- Keep a pot of boiling water on hand for tea drinkers, and offer a variety of herbal and black tea bags. Have on hand milk, lemon wedges, and sweeteners (see below).

- Flavored whipped cream makes a luxurious topping for coffee or hot cocoa. One cup heavy cream makes about $2 1/2$ cups whipped cream.

- *Coffee Whipped Cream:* Pour $1/4$ cup chilled heavy cream into a large bowl. Stir in 2 teaspoons instant coffee or instant espresso powder, 1 tablespoon sugar, and ½ teaspoon pure vanilla extract. Add ¾ cup more cream to the mixture, then whip with an electric mixer or wire whisk until the cream holds stiff peaks.

- *Cocoa Whipped Cream: Pour ⅓ cup chilled heavy cream into a large bowl. Stir in 3 tablespoons unsweetened cocoa powder, 3 tablespoons sugar, ½ teaspoon pure vanilla extract and a pinch of salt. Add ⅔ cup more cream to the mixture, then whip with an electric mixer or wire whisk until the cream holds stiff peaks.*

- *Mocha Whipped Cream: Pour ⅓ cup chilled heavy cream into a large bowl. Stir in 2 teaspoons instant coffee or instant espresso powder, 2 tablespoons unsweetened cocoa powder, 2 tablespoons sugar, and ½ teaspoon pure vanilla extract. Add ⅔ cup more cream to the mixture, then whip with an electric mixer or wire whisk until the cream holds stiff peaks.*

- *Cinnamon Whipped Cream: Pour 1 cup chilled heavy cream into a large bowl. Stir in ½ teaspoon ground cinnamon, 2 tablespoons sugar, and ½ teaspoon pure vanilla extract. Whip with an electric mixer or wire whisk until the cream holds stiff peaks.*

- *Maple Whipped Cream: Pour 1 cup chilled heavy cream into a large bowl. Stir in 2 tablespoons pure maple syrup and ½ teaspoon pure vanilla extract. Whip with an electric mixer or wire whisk until the cream holds stiff peaks.*

- *Almond Whipped Cream: Pour 1 cup chilled heavy cream into a large bowl. Stir in 1 teaspoon almond extract and 1 tablespoon sugar. Whip with an electric mixer or wire whisk until the cream holds stiff peaks.*

- *When it comes to sweeteners, think outside the sugar bowl! Consider offering lump sugar, raw sugar (brown crystals), or superfine sugar for added variety. Rock candy sugar swizzle sticks are another festive option. A pot of honey will make most tea drinkers very happy. You may also want to stock sugar substitutes for those who prefer them.*

Christmas Gifts
from the Kitchen

When I was in college and had little cash to spread around on Christmas gifts, I would bake holiday butter cookies by the dozens and package them in those round tins with cheesy Currier and Ives—like holiday scenes on them. Fact was, people actually appreciated something that was homemade and from the heart. They knew I took the time and effort to make them a one-of-a-kind gift.

Now that I have kids, it's a tradition I want to revive. It's a great family activity and shows that something really neat doesn't have to come from a store. I'm starting to sound like a Dr. Seuss book. And that's not a bad thing.

Orange-Cranberry Bread

The great thing about this bread is the tang of it. It's like having a slice of a big ol' glass of wake-up!

8 tablespoons (1 stick) unsalted butter, softened (page 25)	½ cup orange juice (from 1 to 2 oranges)
1½ cups sugar	1 teaspoon pure vanilla extract
1 large egg	2 cups all-purpose flour
2 teaspoons finely grated orange zest (from 1 orange)	1 teaspoon baking powder
	½ teaspoon salt
	½ cup chopped cranberries

1 • Position a rack in the center of the oven and preheat the oven to 350°F. Butter an 8½ by 4½-inch loaf pan with sides at least 2½ inches high.

2 • Using an electric mixer or mixing by hand, beat together the butter, sugar, and egg until fluffy, about 3 minutes. Add the orange zest, orange juice, and vanilla and mix well. In a small bowl, stir together the flour, baking powder, and salt and add to the butter mixture, beating until just incorporated. Do not overmix. Stir in the cranberries and spoon the batter into the prepared pan.

3 • Bake the bread for 60 to 70 minutes, or until a knife inserted in the center comes out clean. Remove from the oven, place on a wire rack, and let cool for 15 minutes. Meanwhile, make the glaze.

FOR THE GLAZE

⅓ cup confectioners' sugar	2 tablespoons orange juice

1 • In a small bowl, stir together the sugar and orange juice until smooth.

2 • Run a knife around the edges of the pan and invert the bread onto the rack to remove

it from the pan. Place the bread right side up on the rack. Drizzle the glaze on top of the bread while it is still warm. Let the loaf cool completely. Wrapped tightly in plastic wrap, the bread can be stored for up to 4 days at room temperature or frozen for up to 2 months (let thaw before proceeding). Slice and serve.

Makes one 8½ by 4½-inch loaf, or 10 to 12 slices

Banana-Rum Bread

Instead of the traditional fruitcake that has a density and gravity somewhere north of lead, try this Banana-Rum bread. I suggest trying a glass of the rum first to make sure it's really top-notch stuff. Try another to be absolutely certain. All right, thass the lash glash . . . honesht.

8 tablespoons (1 stick) unsalted
    butter, softened (page 25)
1/3 cup sugar
1/3 cup light brown sugar
1 large egg
1 cup mashed banana (from 2 or
    3 bananas)

3 tablespoons rum
1 teaspoon pure vanilla extract
2 cups all-purpose flour
1 teaspoon baking soda
1/2 teaspoon salt
1/2 cup chopped pecans or walnuts,
    toasted (page 23)

1 • Position a rack in the center of the oven, and preheat the oven to 350°F. Butter an 8½ by 4½-inch loaf pan with sides at least 2½ inches high.

2 • Using an electric mixer or mixing by hand, beat together the butter, sugar, and brown sugar until fluffy, about 3 minutes. Add the egg, banana, rum, and vanilla and beat until well combined. In a small bowl, stir together the flour, baking soda, and salt and add to the butter mixture, beating just until incorporated. Do not overmix. Stir in the nuts and spoon the batter into the prepared pan.

3 • Bake the bread for 60 to 70 minutes, or until a knife inserted in the center comes out clean. Remove from the oven, place on a wire rack, and let cool for 15 minutes. Run a knife around the edges of the pan and invert the bread onto the rack to remove it from the pan. Place the bread right side up on the rack and let cool completely. Wrapped tightly in plastic wrap, the bread can be stored for up to 4 days at room temperature or frozen for up to 2 months (let thaw before proceeding). Slice and serve.

Makes one 8½ by 4½-inch loaf, or 10 to 12 slices

Testing Baking Powder and Baking Soda for Freshness

There's nothing worse than following a recipe to a tee, opening the oven, and finding what looks like a pancake where a big fluffy cake ought to be. Okay, having your spleen removed when you checked in for a hangnail might be worse, but the cake disaster is in the Top Ten Worst Things.

To prevent such a baking mishap from befalling you, check expiration dates on baking powder and baking soda at the store before you buy, and store them in airtight containers in a cool, dry place once you're home. Baking powder should be replaced every six to twelve months; baking soda will last nearly indefinitely if properly stored. Use the simple tests below to check boxes and tins of stuff that have been in your cupboard since you can't-remember-when. If they don't pass the test, chuck the stuff and replace it with new baking powder or soda. Finally, remember that while most baking powders are "double acting" (meaning they start working as soon as a batter is mixed and then again when the mixture is heated), baking soda is not (it foams just once, when the batter is made) so for best results get those cakes in a hot oven as soon as you have them ready.

To test baking powder: mix 1 teaspoon baking powder with ½ cup hot water.
To test baking soda: mix ¼ teaspoon baking soda with 2 teaspoons vinegar.

The mixture should bubble and fizz immediately.

Microwave Fudge

In addition to making a fast and easy gift, this is a perfect recipe to make when the urge to splurge on chocolate sneaks up on you. The only way it could be faster would be if your microwave oven could hop down and make it for you. If that happened, I would run like hell, because it would mean Rod Serling was in the house.

3 cups semisweet or milk chocolate chips, or a combination (18 ounces)
1 (14-ounce) can sweetened condensed milk

4 tablespoons (½ stick) unsalted butter, softened (page 25)
2 teaspoons almond extract
1 cup chopped almonds, toasted (page 23)

1 • Lightly butter an 8-inch square pan with sides at least 1½ inches high.

2 • Put the chips in a large, microwave-safe bowl and pour the condensed milk on top. Microwave on high power for 3 minutes. Remove from the microwave oven and stir; the chips should be melted. If not, return to the microwave oven to melt, checking every 30 seconds. Stir until smooth.

3 • Cook the mixture on high for 4 more minutes. Without stirring it, test to see if it has reached the "soft ball stage:" a candy thermometer inserted into the mixture should register 234°F, or a small blob dropped into a cup of ice water should hold together in a squishy ball. If it has not reached this stage, microwave another minute and check again.

4 • Do not stir, but let the chocolate mixture sit until cooled to just warm (about 120°F)—this will take at least 30 minutes. Beat in the butter and the almond extract, stirring vigorously for about 2 minutes until the fudge loses some of its shine. Stir in the nuts.

5 • Spoon the fudge into the prepared pan, using a flat metal spatula or butter knife to smooth the top. Let cool to room temperature, and then cut into 1-inch squares. The fudge can be refrigerated, well wrapped, for up to 1 week or frozen for up to 1 month. Serve at room temperature, chilled, or even frozen (the fudge will have the texture of a frozen candy bar).

Makes sixty-four 1-inch squares

Bourbon Balls

I had my first run-in with Bourbon Balls four years ago when I flew into Louisville, Kentucky, and was greeted by a comely young lady wearing a plantation-era dress and holding a basket of individually wrapped confections. "Bourbon Balls?" she asked. "Mmmm, no. I think they're normal," I replied and walked off. Then I realized what she meant and ran back and apologized.

1 cup vanilla wafer crumbs (about 15 vanilla wafers)
1 cup finely chopped toasted pecans (page 23)
1 cup confectioners' sugar, plus more for rolling cookies

2 tablespoons unsweetened cocoa powder
1½ tablespoons light corn syrup
¼ cup bourbon or rum

1 • In a mixing bowl, stir together the cookie crumbs, pecans, confectioners' sugar, cocoa powder, corn syrup, and bourbon. Scoop the dough out by scant tablespoonfuls and roll into balls. Roll each ball in confectioners' sugar. Place in an airtight container for at least 12 hours for the flavors to develop before serving. The cookies can be stored at room temperature for up to 1 week or frozen, well wrapped, for up to 2 months.

2 • Serve the cookies at room temperature or right from the freezer.

Makes 2 dozen cookies

Basic Sugar Cookies

Okay, this is what I call a triple play. This is a great basic cookie batter that can be the basis for three different cookies. What I like to do is bang out a double batch of dough and freeze one batch. Then I can thaw it later and make another batch of cookies. Or, truth be told, I just eat one quarter of the dough while I'm rolling out the cookies and end up with enough for a batch and a half. You decide what to do with your dough.

---

16 tablespoons (2 sticks) unsalted
   butter, softened (page 25)
1½ cups confectioners' sugar
2 tablespoons light corn syrup
1 large egg
1 large egg yolk

1 tablespoon pure vanilla extract
1 teaspoon finely grated lemon zest
   (from 1 lemon)
3½ cups all-purpose flour
½ teaspoon baking powder
½ teaspoon salt

---

1 • Using an electric mixer or mixing by hand, beat the butter and sugar together until fluffy, about 3 minutes. Add the corn syrup, egg, yolk, vanilla, and lemon zest and beat well. In a small bowl, stir together the flour, baking powder, and salt and add to the butter mixture, mixing just until incorporated.

2 • Gather the dough into a ball and divide the ball in half, flattening each half slightly to form a disk. Cover each disk in plastic wrap or wax paper and refrigerate for at least 1 hour or overnight to firm (if refrigerated for more than an hour, the dough may get too hard to work with easily; let it sit at room temperature, unwrapped, for about 15 minutes to become pliable). You can also freeze the dough, well wrapped, for up to 2 months (thaw before proceeding).

3 • Position 2 racks equidistant apart in the oven. Preheat the oven to 350°F. Lightly butter 2 baking sheets, or line them with parchment paper.

4 • Working with half of the dough (leave the other half in the refrigerator until ready to use), roll it out on a floured board to a ⅛-inch thickness. Cut into desired shapes with cookie cutters and place ½ inch apart on the prepared baking sheets. Gather any

unused scraps into a ball and roll out ⅛ inch thick; cut with cookie cutters. If desired, decorate (see Decorating Unbaked Cookies, page 84).

5 • Bake the cookies for 8 to 10 minutes, switching positions of the baking sheets in the oven halfway through, until just light golden in color.

6 • Remove the cookies from the oven and let rest on the baking sheets for 2 to 3 minutes. Using a metal spatula, carefully remove the cookies from the baking sheets and place them on a wire rack to cool completely.

7 • Repeat with the remaining dough, making sure you let the baking sheets cool completely before proceeding. Decorate as desired (see Decorating Baked Cookies).

8 • Store the cookies at room temperature in an airtight container for up to 5 days, or wrap well and freeze for up to 2 months (let thaw before serving).

Makes about 4 dozen 3-inch cookies

NOTE: When separating an egg to use the yolk, keep the white for another use; cover and refrigerate for up to 24 hours. If you make the Thumbprint Cookies or the Sesame-Date Half-Moons (see pages 86 and 88), or an egg wash for decorating (see Decorating Unbaked Cookies, page 84), you will need the egg white.

Freezing Cookies and Cookie Dough

Most cookie dough can be frozen for up to 2 months. Make sure to wrap it tightly in plastic wrap and thaw completely before using. With a little planning, you can get started early. Then, right before the holidays, do the fun stuff: bake and decorate. You can also freeze baked, unfrosted cookies for 2 months—simply thaw before decorating and serving.

Decorating Unbaked Cookies

- *Press colored sugar, sprinkles, or cinnamon imperials onto the top of the cookies. For extra sticking power, first brush the cookies with an egg white lightly beaten with 1 teaspoon water. (For homemade colored sugar, put 3 tablespoons granulated sugar in a small plastic bag. Add a drop of food coloring, close the bag and rub it between your hands to mix. Add more food coloring for a more intense color.)*
- *An almond, or half a walnut or pecan, makes a nice decoration when pressed in the center of a plain sugar cookie.*

Decorating Baked Cookies

- *Make a glaze by whisking together 2 cups confectioners' sugar, 1 to 2 tablespoons milk, 1 tablespoon melted unsalted butter, and 1 teaspoon vanilla extract. Brush baked and cooled cookies with the glaze, using it as a glue for sprinkles, colored sugar, chopped nuts, or small candies such as mini chocolate or butterscotch chips, candy-coated chocolates, cinnamon imperials, or* crushed candy canes. The glaze is best used soon after it is made; store, if needed, with a piece of plastic wrap pressed right against the surface to prevent a crust from forming, and refrigerate for up to 2 days. Stir well before using.

• Melt chopped chocolate or chocolate chips (page 42) and brush the chocolate in a thick layer onto the cookies. Before the chocolate hardens, sprinkle with chopped, toasted nuts (page 23) if desired. Let the chocolate set before serving.

• Make a cookie sandwich: Before baking, cut cookies of the same size and shape, and cut a tiny shape such as a star, heart or circle out of the centers of half the cookies. Once baked and cooled, spread the whole cookies with a layer of jam (apricot, strawberry, raspberry, or orange marmalade) and press a cut-out cookie on top so that the jam shows through.

• Make decorating icing by mixing 2 cups confectioners' sugar and 1 teaspoon light corn syrup with enough water to make a fluid but thick icing (start with 1 tablespoon water, adding more as need). Add a drop of vanilla, lemon, or almond extract if desired. Leave plain, or add a few drops of food coloring. If you want to use lots of colors, double the recipe and divide the icing among several small bowls, adding a different food coloring to each. Spread the icing on cookies with a table knife or icing spatula, or pipe onto cookies using a pastry bag fitted with a small tip or a plastic bag with a tiny hole cut out of one corner.

Thumbprint Cookies

Until they come up with DNA cookies, these cookies will make a gift that is uniquely yours.

Basic Sugar Cookie dough (pages 82–83)
1 large egg white, lightly beaten
2 cups finely chopped walnuts or
*   pecans, toasted (page 23)*

All-purpose flour, for shaping cookies
1 cup raspberry or strawberry jam, or
*   1 cup melted chocolate (page 42)*

1 • Follow the recipe for Basic Sugar Cookies through step 3.

2 • Working with half of the dough (leave the other half in the refrigerator until ready to use), pinch off about 1 tablespoon and roll it into a ball. Roll the ball in the beaten egg white and then in the chopped nuts. Place the balls on the prepared baking sheets about 1 inch apart. Dip your thumb in flour and create an indentation in the center of each cookie.

3 • Bake for 10 minutes, remove from the oven, and re-imprint the indentation—the dough will be hot, so don't use your thumb this time; the rounded back of a measuring teaspoon works well. Return the cookies to the oven, switching the position of the baking sheets, and bake for 8 to 10 minutes more, until just light golden in color.

4 • Remove the cookies from the oven and let rest on the baking sheets for 2 to 3 minutes. Using a metal spatula, carefully remove the cookies from the baking sheets and place them on a wire rack to cool completely.

5 • Repeat with the remaining dough, making sure you let the baking sheets cool completely before proceeding.

6 • Store unfilled cookies at room temperature in an airtight container for up to 5 days, or wrap well and freeze for up to 2 months (thaw before proceeding).

7 • Fill each "thumbprint" with a generous teaspoon of the jam or melted chocolate, allowing the chocolate to set for 10 minutes or so before serving. The cookies are best served within several hours of filling, but can be stored in an airtight container for up to 1 day.

Makes about 3 dozen cookies

Cinnamon Almond Pinwheels

My mom used to make these cookies. When I was a kid, I could never figure out how she got the pinwheel effect. She told us she spun the cookies really fast. And you wonder why the therapy has taken so long to kick in.

Basic Sugar Cookie dough
    (pages 82–83)
About 3 tablespoons unsalted butter,
    melted

½ cup sugar, plus extra for sprinkling
4 teaspoons ground cinnamon
1 cup finely chopped almonds or
    pecans, toasted (page 23)

1 • Follow the recipe for Basic Sugar Cookies through step 3.

2 • Working with half of the dough (leave the other half in the refrigerator until ready to use), roll it out on a floured board to form a rectangle, approximately 13 inches long, 9 inches wide, and ¼ inch thick.

3 • Using a pastry brush, brush the rectangle with about 2 teaspoons of the melted butter, making sure to brush all the way to the edges. Sprinkle the entire surface with ¼ cup of the sugar, 2 teaspoons cinnamon, and ½ cup chopped nuts. Starting along the long side of the rectangle, begin rolling it up, jelly-roll style, to form a 13-inch-long log. Slice into ¾-inch rounds and place 1 inch apart on the prepared baking sheets. Flatten each round lightly with the palm of your hand. Brush with about 2 more teaspoons butter and sprinkle with additional sugar.

4 • Bake the cookies for 18 to 20 minutes, switching positions of the baking sheets in the oven halfway through, until just light golden in color.

5 • Remove the cookies from the oven and let rest on the baking sheets for 2 to 3 minutes. Using a metal spatula, carefully remove the cookies from the baking sheets and place them on a wire rack to cool completely.

6 • Repeat with the remaining dough, making sure you let the baking sheets cool completely before proceeding.

7 • Store the cookies at room temperature in an airtight container for up to 5 days, or wrap well and freeze for up to 2 months (thaw before serving).

Makes about 3 dozen cookies

Sesame Date Half-Moons

Dates are one of those bizarre fruits that seemed so exotic when you were a kid. Bigger than a raisin, drier than a prune, with a seed that could choke a horse, dates were that sweet, sticky rare treat.

Basic Sugar Cookie dough
    (pages 82–83)
1¼ cups chopped dates (8 ounces)

⅔ cup apricot jam
½ cup sesame seeds
1 large egg white, lightly beaten

1 • Follow the recipe for Basic Sugar Cookies through step 3.

2 • Working with half of the dough (leave the other half in the refrigerator until ready to use), roll it out on a floured board to a ⅛-inch thickness. Cut the dough into 3-inch circles using a round cookie cutter or the floured rim of a drinking glass. Place the dough rounds about 1 inch apart on the prepared baking sheets.

3 • In a small bowl, mix together the dates and jam until well combined. Pour the sesame seeds into a shallow bowl. Spoon a scant teaspoon of the date mixture onto each round of dough, fold the dough over to form a half-circle, and pinch the edges closed with your fingers. Brush the top of each semicircle with the egg white and dip the tops into the sesame seeds. Return the cookies to the baking sheets, sesame seed side up.

4 • Bake the cookies for 18 to 20 minutes, switching positions of the baking sheets in the oven halfway through, until just light golden in color.

5 • Remove the cookies from the oven and let rest on the baking sheets for 2 to 3 minutes. Using a metal spatula, carefully remove the cookies from the baking sheets and place them on a wire rack to cool completely.

6 • Repeat with the remaining dough, making sure you let the baking sheets cool completely before proceeding.

7 • Store the cookies at room temperature in an airtight container for up to 5 days, or wrap well and freeze for up to 2 months (thaw before serving).

Makes about 4 dozen cookies

Packaging Cookies for Gift-Giving

- *Gift containers can be bags, tins, baskets, jars, or boxes. You can also use a paper, plastic, metal, or china plate; set it on a square of plastic wrap or colored cellophane larger than the plate, arrange cookies on top, and then gather up the wrap around the plate to enclose the cookies, securing the wrap with a piece of ribbon, cord, yarn, or a strip of fabric. Trim the package with a sprig of evergreen or holly, a candy cane, or a cookie cutter.*

- *A brand-new baking pan makes the gift last long after the cookies are gone; line it with a sheet of plastic wrap or cellophane that is large enough to gather up around the cookies to protect them. Fasten the wrap, wrap another piece of cellophane around the pan to secures the pan to the cookies, and trim the package as above.*

- *Some cookies ship better than others. Choose medium and small cookies that aren't crumbly or overly moist. Bar cookies also work well. Great choices for mailing include: Basic Sugar Cookies (pages 82–83), Cinnamon Almond Pinwheels (page 87), Sesame Date Half-Moons (see opposite), Platinum Blondies (page 222), Candy Bar Bars (page 223), and Chocolate-Chocolate Cookies (pages 260–61).*

- *To mail cookies: Place a layer of crumpled waxed paper in the bottom of a cookie container, and arrange cookies in a single layer on top. Repeat, ending with a layer of crumpled waxed paper. Tape the cookie container securely shut. Place at least two inches of packing material (such as Styrofoam pellets, crumpled newspaper or tissue paper) into a sturdy box that is larger than the cookie container. Place the cookie container on top of the packing material, and pack more pellets or paper around the sides and top of the container, aiming for about a two-inch buffer all around. Secure the larger box and ship, aiming for delivery within two or three days.*

Homemade Mixes

Here's a super way to give a homemade gift that gives recipients something easy and fun to do, especially if they don't have time to bake from scratch. And if you're partial to making sand sculpture in jars, you can get really creative with the ingredients, layering them to create lovely vistas.

Here are two homemade baking mixes: one is for cookies, the other for gingerbread. Package each recipe in a clean, wide-mouth, one-quart glass canning jar. Label each jar and attach a recipe card with the directions for turning the mix into cookies or gingerbread. The mixes should keep for up to four months if stored in a cool, dry place; refrigeration is not necessary.

TOFFEE-CHIP COOKIES-IN-A-JAR

½ cup packed dark brown sugar
½ cup packed light brown sugar
½ cup milk chocolate toffee candy bits (available in the baking aisle of the supermarket) or 2 (1.4-ounce) milk chocolate toffee bars, crushed

1½ cups all-purpose flour
½ teaspoon salt
½ teaspoon baking powder
1¼ cups semisweet chocolate chips (8 ounces)

1 • Carefully spoon each ingredient, in order, into a clean, wide-mouth quart jar, making sure to pack down the dark and light brown sugars. Close the jar lid tightly. Label the jar, and, on a recipe card, write the following directions for mixing and baking:

2 • Position 2 racks equidistant apart in the oven. Preheat the oven to 350°F. Lightly butter 2 baking sheets, or line them with parchment paper.

3 • Using an electric mixer or mixing by hand, beat together:

12 tablespoons (1½ sticks) unsalted butter, softened (page 25)

1 large egg
1 teaspoon pure vanilla extract

4 • Add the cookie mix and stir to combine. Scoop 1 tablespoon of the dough and roll it into a ball. Place on a prepared baking sheet and flatten slightly with the palm of your hand. Repeat with the remaining dough, setting the cookies about 2 inches apart.

5 • Bake the cookies for 12 to 14 minutes, switching the position of the baking sheets halfway through, until lightly browned. Let the cookies set on the baking sheets for 2 to 3 minutes. Using a metal spatula, carefully remove the cookies from the baking sheets and place them on a wire rack to cool completely.

Makes about 2½ dozen cookies

GINGERBREAD-IN-A-JAR

The flour in this recipe is divided so that the spices create a colorful layer in the jar.

¾ cup packed dark brown sugar
½ cup sugar
1 cup all-purpose flour
1 tablespoon ground ginger
2 teaspoons instant coffee granules
    (preferably instant espresso powder)

1 teaspoon ground cinnamon
1 teaspoon ground cloves
½ teaspoon salt
1½ cups all-purpose flour

1 • Carefully spoon each ingredient, in order, into a clean, wide-mouth quart jar, making sure to pack down the brown sugar. Close the jar lid tightly. Label the jar, and, on a recipe card, write the following directions for mixing and baking:

2 • Position a rack in the center of the oven and preheat the oven to 350°F. Lightly butter a 9 by 13-inch baking pan with sides at least 1½ inches high.

3 • Using an electric mixer or mixing by hand, beat together:

8 tablespoons (1 stick) unsalted
butter, at room temperature

1 cup unsulphured molasses
2 large eggs

4 • Add the gingerbread mix and 1 cup boiling water and stir to combine.

5 • Pour the batter into the prepared pan and bake for 35 to 40 minutes, or until a knife inserted in the center of the cake comes out clean. Place the pan on a wire rack, and let cool at least partially before serving. Cut into 3-inch squares. Sprinkle with confectioners' sugar, if desired, and serve warm or at room temperature, plain or with whipped cream or ice cream.

Makes twelve 3-inch squares

TO DECORATE THE JARS: Cut an 8-inch circle of fabric with pinking shears and place over jar lid. Secure with a rubber band, and then tie with attractive ribbon, raffia, yarn, or fabric strips. If you punch a hole in the recipe card, you can tie it to the jar lid with the ribbon.

Vanilla-Cinnamon Party Nuts

Okay, before you give these out, you have to make sure that nobody's allergic to nuts, or else their head explodes and that does NOT put people in the festive holiday spirit.

---

2 large egg whites, at room temperature
1 cup sugar
¼ teaspoon salt

1 tablespoon pure vanilla extract
1 teaspoon ground cinnamon
4 cups pecans or walnuts, or a mixture of both, toasted (page 23)

---

1 • Position a rack in the center of the oven and preheat the oven to 250°F. Line a baking sheet with parchment paper.

2 • In a large, very clean bowl (any trace of grease will keep the whites from whipping to their fullest volume), whip the egg whites with an electric mixer on high speed until they hold soft peaks. Add the sugar, salt, vanilla, and cinnamon and beat on low speed until just mixed. Stir in the nuts and toss until well coated. Transfer the nuts to the baking sheet and spread them out in a single layer.

3 • Bake, stirring gently every 15 minutes, until the nuts are golden, about 40 minutes.

4 • Remove the pan from the oven and set it on a wire rack to cool. After 5 minutes, remove the nuts with a metal spatula and spread them out on a cutting board to cool completely. The nuts can be stored at room temperature in an airtight container for up to 1 week.

Makes 4 cups

Caribbean Spice Mix

Spicy is the buzz word these days. Everybody likes a little kick in their seasoning. Well, here's something from the CARIBBEAN that will be no problem, mon.

¼ cup packed dark brown sugar	2 tablespoons dried thyme leaves
¼ cup hot red pepper flakes	4 teaspoons ground allspice
2 tablespoons garlic powder	2 teaspoons ground cinnamon
2 tablespoons coarse salt	1 teaspoon freshly ground pepper

In a small bowl, stir together all of the ingredients. Spoon into an 8-ounce jar, or two 4-ounce jars. Close the jar lid tightly and label, with suggestions for use such as: "Excellent as a rub on pork, poultry, or fish. Or use as a flavoring for soups and stews." This mix will keep indefinitely at room temperature, but is best used within 6 months.

Makes 1 cup

Boxing Day:
A Caribbean Menu

I first learned about Boxing Day when I was doing one of those projects we've all done in elementary school. I was in fifth grade at St. Catherine of Sienna School in St. Albans, New York. We all had to write a few paragraphs about Christmas traditions in the land of our ancestors.

My dad's mother and father were from the Bahamas, while my mother's family was from Jamaica. I chose to talk to Grandma Roker, since she still went back to Nassau and her home island of Exuma quite a bit.

It was Grandma Roker who told me about Boxing Day. Since the Bahamas had been a British Colony since the 1600s, many of their traditions were gleaned from the United Kingdom. In fact, when I first went there, in 1967, they still flew the Union Jack flag along with the Bahamian flag, and the day I landed, the Queen's Birthday was in full celebration.

Grandma Roker told me that Boxing Day was celebrated the day after Christmas. The plantation owners would box up leftover food and presents, wrap them in the remains of the wrapping papers that had festooned their gifts, and the overseers would distribute them amongst the slaves. Hence, Boxing Day.

It was also one of the few times that the slaves would be given twenty-four hours off. They might spend it visiting with family or friends at other plantations. Boxing Day observations survived the test of time and are still observed all over the Caribbean.

A bittersweet holiday for those of us who hail from the Islands, Boxing Day is still a celebration. It is also a chance to explain the misery and the inhumanity of slavery to our children. A few years back, Courtney and I took a trip to Exuma and saw the slave quarters where my grandparents' ancestors were kept, packed like cattle. You can never know how far you've come, without knowing where you've come from.

Yet, we survived and we've thrived and the tradition of Boxing Day lives on. Here is a taste of the Islands when the snow is blowing and the warmth of spring and summer seems so far away.

Tropical Punch

When I was a lad, there was a commercial on TV in which a little wise guy would ask this unsuspecting boob, "Hey, how about a nice Hawaiian punch?" "Sure," the sap would answer, and the wise guy would bust him right in the mush.

Of course, who knows if that stuff was made in Hawaii.

But I have had a version of this punch in the CARIBBEAN. And there, nobody tries to rearrange your dental work when they ask you if you'd like one.

¼ cup water
¼ cup sugar
1 (1-quart, 14-ounce) can pineapple juice
2 cups bottled apricot nectar
2 cups orange juice (from 6 to 7 oranges)

¾ cup lemon juice (from 3 to 4 lemons)
¼ cup lime juice (from 2 to 3 limes)
2 mangoes, optional
1 liter ginger ale, chilled
Ice cubes, for serving

1 • Stir together the water and sugar in a small saucepan over medium-high heat. Bring to a boil, reduce the heat, and simmer for 2 minutes, stirring occasionally to dissolve the sugar. Let cool, then cover and refrigerate for up to 1 month.

2 • In a 1-gallon pitcher, combine the sugar syrup, pineapple juice, apricot nectar, orange juice, lemon juice, and lime juice. If desired, pour off 2 cups of the mixture and freeze it in ice cube trays. Cover and refrigerate the remaining punch until thoroughly chilled, at least 2 hours and up to 24 hours.

3 • Peel the mangoes, and slice as much pulp as you can off the pits. Puree the pulp, along with several cups of the punch, in a blender, and strain it into the punch.

4 • Pour the chilled punch into a punch bowl and gently stir in the ginger ale. Add the frozen punch or regular ice cubes. If desired, place a bottle of rum near the punch bowl for any adults who want a stronger drink.

Makes 1 gallon, or about twenty 6-ounce servings

NOTE: You may want to make a double, triple, or quadruple batch of sugar syrup. It keeps well, and is a wonderful sweetener for iced tea, iced coffee, or homemade lemonade.

Twice-Fried Plantains
with Green Salsa

When I was growing up here in New York City, we knew about plantains, but outside of, say, NYC or Los Angeles, you'd have been hard pressed to find them far from areas where mostly Spanish-speaking folks lived. Well, with the Latin Flava being so hot right now, you can find everything Latin in almost every grocery store in America, including these green cousins of the banana. A tip: serve 'em right away by passing 'em around on a platter.

FOR THE SALSA

1 green bell pepper, stemmed, seeded, and finely chopped
2 jalapeño peppers, stemmed, seeded, and finely chopped
½ small onion, peeled and finely chopped
1 clove garlic, peeled and finely chopped

¼ cup chopped cilantro leaves
2 tablespoons canola or other vegetable oil
1 tablespoon lime juice (from 1 lime)
½ teaspoon salt

Mix all of the ingredients together in a small bowl. Cover and refrigerate for at least 1 hour and up to 24 hours.

FOR THE PLANTAINS

3 cups peanut or canola oil
4 green plantains (about 2 pounds)

Coarse salt

1 • Heat the oil in a deep skillet or a wide saucepan until it reaches 325°F to 350°F on a candy or deep-fry thermometer. Line 2 baking sheets or platters with several layers of paper towels.

2 • While the oil is heating, cut each plantain crosswise in half. Using a paring knife, slit the skin lengthwise and pull it off. Cut the plantains into 1-inch-thick rounds.

3 • Using a slotted spoon, and without crowding the pan, carefully drop 4 or 5 plantain slices at a time into the hot oil (the oil may splatter) and fry until light golden but not browned, 4 to 5 minutes. Remove the slices with a slotted spoon and place them on one of the prepared baking sheets. Repeat with the remaining plantains, regulating the heat as much as possible to keep the temperature constant.

4 • When all the slices are fried, flatten each piece with the bottom of a skillet, a small cutting board, or the broad side of a cleaver. Drop the flattened slices, in batches, back into the hot oil. Fry until golden brown, another 4 to 5 minutes. Drain on the other prepared baking sheet. Sprinkle immediately with coarse salt and serve hot, topped with the salsa.

Makes 8 servings

Chicken Pilau

It's a good thing those plantation owners didn't have this recipe. If they had, there would have been no leftovers for those Boxing Day boxes!

4 to 5 pounds chicken pieces (see note)
1/2 cup sugar
1/4 cup canola oil or other vegetable oil
1 cup canned unsweetened coconut milk
3 cups canned chicken broth, or more as needed
2 (15 1/2-ounce) cans pigeon peas or black-eyed peas, rinsed and drained
2 cups white rice

2 carrots, peeled and cut into 1/4-inch rounds
1 large onion, peeled and cut into 1/4-inch pieces
1 green bell pepper, stemmed, seeded, and cut into 1/4-inch pieces
1/4 cup ketchup
Salt
Freshly ground pepper
8 scallions, white and green parts, chopped
1/4 cup chopped parsley leaves

1 • Rinse the chicken under cold running water and pat dry with paper towels.

2 • Stir together the sugar and oil in a large, heavy pot over medium-high heat. Cook until the mixture liquefies and begins to turn deep brown, 2 to 3 minutes. Add the chicken and turn so that each piece is well coated. Cook until each piece is well browned, about 4 minutes on each side. Add the coconut milk and broth, reduce the heat to medium, and cook, covered, for about 15 minutes.

3 • Stir in the peas, rice, carrots, onion, bell pepper, and ketchup and season with salt and pepper. Reduce the heat to medium-low and simmer until the rice is tender and most of the liquid has been absorbed, about 30 minutes. Remove a piece of chicken and slice into the center to make sure it is no longer pink (an instant read thermometer inserted into the thickest part of the meat should read 170°F). If the chicken is still pink, return it to the pot, and cook the stew a bit longer, checking for doneness at 5-minute intervals. Add more chicken broth if the stew seems too dry. The stew can be cooled, covered, and refrigerated for up to 24 hours or frozen, well wrapped, for up to 1 month (reheat gently before serving).

4 • Add the scallions and parsley to the hot stew and stir well. Ladle into warm, shallow bowls, making sure each serving contains some chicken, rice, and vegetables. Pass a bottle of hot sauce at the table.

Makes 8 to 10 servings

NOTE: The chicken parts should be more or less the same size, so that they cook in about the same amount of time. A combination of thighs and bone-in chicken breast halves, cut in half crosswise, works well.

Caribbean Christmas Cake

My Grandma Roker made this cake most Christmases and we loved it. This is what we knew as fruitcake, so we never understood why people were always dissing THEIR aunts' or grandmothers' fruitcakes. Then, I tried a fruitcake that a college roommate's well-meaning grandmother had sent. Whoa!! Who sent the Rosetta Stone and passed it off as pastry?

Try this version. You'll see why Remilda Roker had it goin' on long before they even knew what it meant.

1½ cups raisins
1 cup currants
1 cup chopped dried pineapple
¾ cup chopped pitted prunes
1¾ cups ruby port
6 tablespoons light rum
2 cups all-purpose flour
1 tablespoon baking powder
¾ teaspoon salt
1½ teaspoons ground nutmeg

½ teaspoon ground cinnamon
¼ teaspoon ground allspice
16 tablespoons (2 sticks) unsalted
    butter, softened (page 25)
6 tablespoons packed light brown
    sugar
4 large eggs
2 tablespoons unsulphured molasses
1 tablespoon pure vanilla extract
1 tablespoon lime juice (from 1 lime)

---

1 • Combine the raisins, currants, pineapple, and prunes in a large saucepan over medium-low heat. Stir in 1½ cups of the port and 4 tablespoons (¼ cup) of the rum. Simmer over low heat for 15 minutes. Remove from the heat and set aside to cool. If not baking the cake immediately, cover and refrigerate for up to 3 days. Combine the remaining ¼ cup port and 2 tablespoons rum in a jar, cover, and set aside.

2 • Position a rack in the center of the oven and preheat the oven to 350°F. Butter a 9-inch, preferably springform, tube pan. Line the bottom with a ring of parchment paper, and butter the parchment.

3 • In a bowl, stir together the flour, baking powder, salt, nutmeg, cinnamon, and allspice. Set aside.

4 • Using an electric mixer or mixing by hand, beat together the butter, brown sugar, eggs,

molasses, vanilla, and lime juice. Add half the flour mixture and stir well. Add all of the soaked fruits (with any remaining liquid) and stir. Add the remaining flour mixture and stir very well until completely combined. Spoon the batter into the prepared pan (it will be about two-thirds full).

5 • Bake the cake for 1 hour and 15 minutes, or until a knife inserted in the center comes out clean.

6 • Remove the cake from the oven, and place upright on a wire rack to cool in the pan for 15 to 20 minutes. Run a knife around the sides of the pan and around the tube. If using a regular tube pan, invert the cake, remove the pan, peel off the parchment and turn the cake upright on the rack. If using a springform tube pan, simply remove the sides; you can remove the bottom, if desired, or you can let the cake sit on the bottom for serving.

7 • While the cake is still warm, place it on a serving plate and poke 6 or 8 holes in the top of the cake with a toothpick or skewer. Slowly pour the remaining port-rum mixture over the top of the cake, letting it seep into the holes.

8 • The cake can be served the day it is made, but, like most fruitcakes, it gets better as it sits. Store, well wrapped, at room temperature for up to 3 weeks. Slice and serve.

Makes one 9-inch tube cake, or at least 12 servings

New Year's Eve
Retro Cocktail Party

Put a little Sammy Davis, Jr., Lou Rawls, or Ol' Blue Eyes on the turntable, bring out your silver sharkskin suit, and let's have us an old-fashioned cocktail party.

I remember my folks having a few of these when I was around six or seven. It was the early sixties and cocktail parties were still all the rage. My folks had a cocktail shaker, martini set, all the highball and cocktail glasses. And, of course, the booze. Yep, and cigarettes and all the stuff that we thought was cool before we knew better.

It was always a great evening. My mother would start early in the day making hors d'oeuvres and appetizers. Then by seven o'clock, Dad would get home and I'd start smelling her perfume and his cologne as they transformed from Mom and Dad to Isabel and Al, couple about town. All of their friends that I always saw in bus uniforms or nurses outfits showed up at the appointed hour dressed to the nines.

I remember that, before the party, my mom put out a big bowl of candy chocolate stars as she got the apartment ready for the evening's festivities. I kept snitching chocolate stars. Finally she looked at me and yelled, "Albert Lincoln Roker! If you eat one more of those, you're going to turn into a chocolate star!"

So I stayed away from them for about an hour. Eventually, I forgot her warning and popped one into my mouth. Just as I was swallowing I remembered what she said. Now

I was deathly afraid to fall asleep, lest I awaken as a fifty-pound chocolate star nestled on my pillow.

Who knew that, forty-three years later, I'd be . . . a chocolate star! And you'll be the star of the cocktail party set if you fix some of these recipes.

Pigs in a Blanket (page 122), Shrimp with Cocktail Sauce (page 120), Biscuits with Ham and Apple Butter (page 119), and Classic Cocktails (page 107)

Chicken Pilau (page 100)
with Tropical Punch (page 97)

Smoked Beef Ribs with
Mustard Sauce (page 226)

Glazed Baked Ham (page 180)
with Roasted Baby Potatoes (page 185)

*Grilled Glazed Doughnuts
with Vanilla Ice Cream (page 236)*

Stovetop Clambake (page 242)

Oven-Fried Chicken with Pecan-Cornmeal Crust
(page 218), Three-Bean Salad (page 221), and
Fizzy Raspberry Lemonade (page 216)

Chopped Summer Salad (page 235)

Pasta Primavera (page 148)

Carrot Cupcakes with Lemony
Cream Cheese Frosting (page 258)
and Caramel Apples (page 262)

Meaty Chili (page 135)
with Corn and Cheese Muffins (page 137)

Chocolate Pecan Pie (page 40)

Roast Turkey and Gravy (page 12),
Corn Bread Stuffing for a Crowd (page 22),
and Fresh Cranberry Relish (page 36)

Red and Green Christmas Salad (page 53)

Red Velvet Cake (page 64)
and Eggnog (page 48)

Platinum Blondies (page 222), Thumbprint Cookies (page 86), Chocolate-Chocolate Cookies (page 260), Microwave Fudge (page 80), Candy Bar Bars (page 223), and Cinnamon Almond Pinwheels (page 87)

Classic Cocktails

Cocktail purists and professional bartenders chill cocktail glasses by filling them with ice (cracked ice works faster than cubes) and letting them stand for a few minutes while they mix the drinks. Discard the cracked ice or, if leaving it in the glass, drain any melted ice before you pour in the drink to avoid diluting it. But an unchilled glass is just fine at home, too.

Martini: For each cocktail, combine in a shaker 2 ounces gin and ½ ounce dry (white) vermouth. Add ice and shake. Strain into a martini glass. Garnish with a twist of lemon or a pitted green olive.

Singapore Sling: For each cocktail, combine in a shaker 2 ounces gin, ¾ ounce apricot brandy, ¾ ounce cherry brandy, a dash of orange-flavored liqueur, juice of ½ lime, and 1 teaspoon sugar. Add ice and shake to mix. Strain into a highball glass. Add ice and chilled seltzer or ginger ale to fill the glass.

Old-Fashioned: For each cocktail, combine in an old-fashioned glass 1 teaspoon sugar, 3 dashes bitters, and 1 teaspoon water. Stir to dissolve the sugar. Add 2 ounces rye whiskey or bourbon. Add ice and stir gently. Garnish with a slice of orange, a slice of pineapple, and a maraschino cherry.

Sidecar: For each cocktail, stir together in an old-fashioned glass 2 ounces brandy, 1 ounce orange-flavored liqueur, and 1 ounce lemon juice. Serve straight up or over ice, with a twist of lemon and a maraschino cherry.

Stinger: For each cocktail, combine in a cocktail shaker 2 ounces brandy, rum, gin, tequila or vodka, 2 ounces white crème de menthe, and 1 ounce lime juice. Add ice and shake vigorously. Strain into an old-fashioned glass and serve straight up with a twist of lime.

Fuzzy Navel: For each cocktail, combine over ice in a highball glass 3 ounces peach schnapps and 3 ounces orange juice. Stir gently and garnish with orange slices.

Manhattan: For each cocktail, combine in a shaker 1½ ounces whiskey, ¾ ounce red (sweet) vermouth, and a dash of orange bitters. Add ice and shake gently. Strain into a cocktail glass; garnish with a twist of lemon or a maraschino cherry.

Cocktail Talk

With a twist: Served with a thin strip of lemon, lime, or orange peel (adds citrus flavor to the drink), twisted over or put directly into the glass. Remove the peel from the fruit with a vegetable peeler or a sharp paring knife, avoiding as much of the bitter white pith as possible.

On the rocks: Served over ice cubes.

Up or straight up: Served without ice.

Virgin: A cocktail served without alcohol.

Free pour: Splashing ingredients into a shaker or glass without measuring.

Highball: Alcohol and a mixer (club soda, juice) served in a tall glass.

Make-Ahead Drink Garnishes

When you need lots of citrus slices to finish off cocktails, make and freeze them ahead. Slice lemons, limes, or oranges, lay flat on a cookie sheet lined with parchment or wax paper and freeze. Once frozen, pop the slices in a plastic bag and return to the freezer. Not only do they flavor and decorate drinks, they also serve as ice cubes.

Cocktail Party Math

Drinks: Plan on one drink per person per hour of your party. If you offer a full bar, have at least one bottle each of vodka, rum, scotch, bourbon, tequila, gin, and brandy. You may need some bitters (and orange bitters as well) and grenadine. Buy plenty of mixers (juice, seltzer, tonic water, tomato juice, and sodas) for cocktails and for those who don't want alcohol. Many of your guests will appreciate wine, beer, or sparkling cider.

Ice: Remember to make or buy plenty of ice cubes. You might also want to consider keeping some cracked ice on hand (see Cocktail Party Equipment, opposite).

Glasses: You'll need at least two kinds of cocktail glasses (see Cocktail Equipment, opposite): highball or double-old-fashioned glasses and martini or stemmed cocktail glasses. If serving wine or champagne, stock the appropriate glasses as well. Count on each guest trading a dirty glass for a clean one at least once. For a large party, plastic glasses are a lifesaver; but if you want real glasses and don't own enough, rent them—you even get to return them unwashed!

Food: Plan on each guest eating at least five hors d'oeuvres per hour for the first two hours of the party, and three hors d'oeuvres per hour after that. Supplement the prepared hors d'oeuvres with bowls of nuts, popcorn, and chips. (See Ten Things to Put on a Cracker, page 118, and No-Cook Hors d'Oeuvres for a Crowd, pages 8–9.)

Cocktail Party Equipment

Jigger: A measuring device as well as a unit of measure. A standard jigger is 1½ ounces. The most versatile jiggers measure not only a standard jigger but a half-jigger (¾ ounce) and a pony (1 ounce). If you don't have a jigger, use measuring spoons: remember that 1 tablespoon equals ½ ounce, 2 tablespoons equals 1 ounce, and so on.

Cocktail Shaker: A mixing container equipped with a screw top and pouring spout. Purists prefer a glass shaker, because glass won't affect the flavor of the drink like some metals will. If you don't have a cocktail shaker, use a jar with a lid.

Strainer: A wire strainer that clips onto the rim of the shaker and allows you to strain the shaken cocktail into a glass.

Ice Crusher or Blender (for cracked ice): The many surfaces of cracked ice cool a drink faster. Some blenders can crush ice (check your owner's manual) or you can seal cubes in a sturdy, plastic freezer bag and whack them with a rolling pin. Drain the cracked ice before using to avoid diluting the drinks.

Stirrer: A glass rod or long handled spoon used for mixing cocktails.

Glassware:
- Classic cocktail or martini glass: A 3- to 4-ounce, flared, stemmed glass.
- Old-fashioned glass: A 6- to 8-ounce tumbler.
- Double old-fashioned: A 15- to 16-ounce tumbler
- Collins glass: A 10- to 14-ounce, straight-sided tall glass
- Highball glass: An 8-ounce, straight-sided glass

Finishes: Check your local party-supply store for paper umbrellas, swizzle sticks, straws, and plastic spears (for garnishes). Edible decorations include maraschino cherries; half-slices of lemons, limes, and oranges; green olives; pickled onions; chunks of pineapple; and fresh or frozen raspberries.

Other Equipment: Ice bucket, tongs, corkscrew, bottle opener, lemon and lime squeezer, paring knife, and small cutting board. Don't forget plenty of paper napkins, small plates, cutlery, toothpicks for spearing hors d'oeuvres, and coasters.

Champagne Cocktails

One 750-milliliter bottle of champagne will make 5 to 7 drinks. You can chill champagne glasses by filling them with ice for a few minutes (discard before adding champagne), but unchilled glasses are perfectly fine.

Kir Royale: For each cocktail, combine 5 ounces chilled champagne and 1 ounce crème de cassis in a glass. Garnish with 2 or 3 fresh raspberries, if desired.

Classic Champagne Cocktail: For each cocktail, put 1 teaspoon sugar, 1 teaspoon brandy, and 3 dashes bitters into a glass. Stir to dissolve the sugar. Add 4 to 6 ounces chilled champagne and stir gently.

Mimosa: For each cocktail, combine ¼ cup orange juice and 4 ounces chilled champagne in a glass.

Champagne Cup: For each cocktail, gently stir together 4 ounces chilled champagne and ½ ounce brandy. Add ice and garnish with a slice of orange, a strawberry or cherry, and a sprig of fresh mint.

Champagne Julep: For each cocktail, spoon 1 teaspoon sugar and a sprig of fresh mint into a glass and add 4 ounces chilled champagne, stirring gently to dissolve the sugar. Add ice and stir again.

Garlicky Cheese Dip

When you're having cool, refreshing beverages, you need to have something to go with those cool, refreshing beverages. I find a cheesy, salty dip is just the ticket. But these days, we like our snacks to have a little kick, a little bite. A dip that breaks through the cool, refreshing beverage.

Garlic breaks through. Feta cheese, with its salty bite breaks through. And with garlicky, cheesy breath, you'll break through as well. Don't worry about people shunning you. This dip will be snarfed up by everyone, so you'll all have garlicky, cheesy breath. Say, that sounds like a reason to have another cool, refreshing beverage!!!

2 cups regular or low-fat cottage cheese (16 ounces)
1 cup crumbled feta cheese (4 ounces)
2 tablespoons extra-virgin olive oil
1 tablespoon lemon juice

2 large cloves garlic, peeled and chopped
1 teaspoon dried oregano
1 cup chopped, pitted black olives
2 tablespoons chopped parsley leaves

1 • In a blender, combine the cottage cheese, feta, olive oil, lemon juice, garlic, and oregano. Puree until smooth. Scrape into a bowl and stir in the olives and parsley. Cover and refrigerate for at least 1 hour and up to 2 days. Stir well before serving.

2 • Serve with raw vegetables, thick potato chips, bagel chips, or pita wedges for dipping.

Makes about 3 cups

Hot Crab Dip

There is nothing low fat about this dish. Yet once you try it, you don't care. I always thought it would make a great sandwich. Just make sure you've got a registered nurse and a defibrillator standing by.

---

8 ounces cream cheese, softened
½ cup mayonnaise
1 tablespoon lemon juice (from 1 lemon)
¼ teaspoon hot sauce
3 scallions, white and green parts,
    chopped

12 ounces lump crabmeat (2 cups)
Salt
Freshly ground pepper
2 to 3 tablespoons freshly grated
    Parmesan cheese

---

1 • Position a rack in the center of the oven and preheat the oven to 400°F.

2 • In a large bowl, using a wooden spoon, mix together the cream cheese and mayonnaise until light and fluffy. Stir in the lemon juice, hot sauce, and scallions and gently fold in the crabmeat. Season with salt and pepper. The crab mixture can be covered and refrigerated for up to 24 hours.

3 • Transfer the dip to a 3-cup, ovenproof dish. Sprinkle with the Parmesan and bake until bubbly and golden, 15 to 20 minutes.

4 • Serve hot or warm with bagel chips, sliced French bread, or pumpernickel rounds for dipping.

Makes about 2½ cups

Cheese Straws

These are to be served at any self-respecting cocktail party. But the best thing is, they're pretty easy thanks to the ready-made frozen puff pastry.

2 (10-inch square) sheets frozen puff pastry (one 17.3-ounce package), thawed according to package directions

1 large egg, well beaten
4 ounces freshly grated Parmesan cheese (1 cup)
2 teaspoons freshly ground pepper

1 • Position a rack in the center of the oven and preheat the oven to 400°F. Lightly butter 2 baking sheets, or line them with parchment paper.

2 • On a lightly floured work surface, roll out 1 sheet of puff pastry until it is approximately 11 inches wide and 16 inches long. Cover and refrigerate the other sheet of pastry until needed.

3 • Using a pastry brush, coat the entire surface with some of the beaten egg. Sprinkle with ¼ cup of the Parmesan and 1 teaspoon of the pepper. Fold the sheet in half crosswise, so that the edges meet. Roll out again until you have formed an 11 by 16-inch rectangle. Brush the surface with egg, sprinkle with ¼ cup of the cheese and press the cheese into the pastry with your hands.

4 • Using a sharp knife or a pizza cutter, cut 11-inch-long strips of puff pastry, ¾ to 1 inch wide. You should be able to cut 16 to 20 strips from 1 sheet. Twist the strips loosely 5 or 6 times, from the center out, and place them on the prepared baking sheets. Press the straws' tips to the pan so they don't shrink. Repeat the entire process with the remaining pastry, egg, cheese, and pepper. The cheese straws can be covered with plastic wrap and frozen. Once frozen (about 2 hours), transfer the cheese straws to an airtight container and freeze for up to 1 month.

5 • Bake the cheese straws for 10 to 12 minutes (1 or 2 minutes longer, if frozen), until golden in color.

6 • Remove from the oven and transfer the cheese straws to a wire rack to cool.

7 • These are best served the day they are made but can be kept, well wrapped, for up to 3 days.

Makes about 36 cheese straws

VARIATIONS

Herbed Cheese Straws

Add 1 tablespoon dried oregano, 1 tablespoon dried basil, and 2 teaspoons garlic powder to the Parmesan cheese and stir to mix well.

Spicy Jack Cheese Straws

Substitute 1 cup finely grated Monterey Jack cheese for the Parmesan. Just before cutting the pastry, sprinkle each sheet of pastry with 1½ teaspoons chili powder and 1 tablespoon chopped cilantro leaves, pressing the topping into the pastry sheets with your hands.

Pistachio Cheese Straws

Finely chop ¼ cup pistachio nuts. Just before cutting the pastry, sprinkle 2 tablespoons of the chopped nuts over each pastry sheet, pressing them into the pastry with your hands.

Ten Things to Put on a Cracker

Pick up your favorite cracker. Look at it. Turn it around in your hand. Does it look like a ready-made snack? Not really. But with our Al Roker's Hassle-Free Holiday Top Ten Things to Put on a Cracker, you have the makings of a quick, easy snack to delight and amaze your friends.

The key here is quality ingredients. Stuff that's been sitting in the bargain bin for months isn't gonna cut it. Hey, you're saving a ton o' time with the crackers. So spend some of that time getting the toppings right.

- *Cream cheese, mango chutney, and currants*
- *Cream cheese and smoked trout or mackerel*
- *Ricotta cheese, pesto, and a sliver of tomato*
- *Frozen lima beans, thawed and cooked according to package directions and pureed with a splash of olive oil and hot sauce*
- *Creamy blue cheese and bits of crisp bacon*
- *Creamy blue cheese and thinly sliced apple or pear*
- *Creamy blue cheese and toasted walnut or pecan halves (page 23)*
- *Hummus and jarred, drained roasted red pepper*
- *Herbed goat cheese and drained, oil-packed sun-dried tomatoes*
- *Deviled ham and a slice of sweet pickle or pickled okra*

Biscuits with Ham and Apple Butter

Apple butter is one of those treats that I associate with childhood. Hot biscuits or toast and that thick, pungent, rust-colored sweet spread of apple butter transforms any bread into a yummy sensation.

¼ cup mayonnaise	Baking Powder Biscuits, preferably
2 tablespoons Dijon mustard	variation made with cheese
¼ pound thinly sliced ham, prefer-	(page 29)
ably smoked or honey-baked	1¼ cups apple butter

1 • In a small bowl, mix together the mayonnaise and mustard. Set aside.

2 • Stack 3 thin slices of ham on top of each other and cut into 2-inch rounds using a biscuit cutter or a sharp knife. You'll need 18 to 20 rounds.

3 • Split each biscuit. Spread about 1 tablespoon of apple butter on the bottom half and top with a ham round. Spread some of the mayonnaise mixture on the cut surface of the top half of the biscuit and put on top of the ham. Serve immediately or cover with plastic wrap and keep at room temperature for up to 2 hours.

Makes 18 to 20 small sandwiches

Shrimp with Cocktail Sauce

I remember my first shrimp cocktail. (Why can I remember my first time trying certain foods and not my first kiss? Just one more question for the therapist.) It was one of those bottled cocktails. My mother had gotten some for a cocktail party she was having. I snitched one and pried the lid off. Wow!! The cocktail sauce, sweet yet spicy and the shrimp were, to my then untrained palate, delicious. It was a cocktail party in my mouth.

Well, today, you could make your own sauce using the recipe below, or you can doctor up some store-bought. I think you have to decide where you want to spend the time. I don't think you'll lose points. I won't tell if you don't. If you want to doctor up store-bought cocktail sauce, here are some things you could add: hot sauce, bottled grated white horseradish, Asian chili paste, grated lemon zest, lemon juice, grated onion, finely chopped garlic, celery seed, and Worcestershire sauce.

3 pounds large (26 to 30 count) fresh or frozen cooked, shelled shrimp or 3½ pounds fresh or frozen raw shrimp
½ cup ketchup
½ cup bottled chili sauce
¼ cup bottled grated white horse-radish, drained

1 tablespoon lemon juice (from 1 lemon)
1 clove garlic, peeled and minced
½ teaspoon celery seeds
1 teaspoon Worcestershire sauce
Salt
Freshly ground pepper

1 • For shrimp that is already cooked, thaw if necessary and keep refrigerated until you are ready to serve.

2 • For raw shrimp—fresh or frozen (and thawed)—cook by placing the shrimp in a pot with just enough water to cover them. Cover the pot and bring the water to a boil. Reduce the heat and simmer just until the shrimp turn pink, 2 to 3 minutes. Drain the shrimp in a colander and immediately run them under cold water to stop the cooking. Peel the shrimp (keep the tails on if desired) and devein them by running a sharp knife

along the vein and removing it. (Or you can skip the deveining process; the vein won't hurt you.) Refrigerate until well chilled, at least 2 hours and up to 24 hours.

3 • In a medium bowl, mix together the ketchup, chili sauce, horseradish, lemon juice, garlic, celery seeds, and Worcestershire sauce. Season with salt and pepper. Cover and refrigerate until well chilled, at least 1 hour and up to 2 days.

4 • To serve, spoon the cocktail sauce into a small bowl and place it in the center of a large platter. Arrange the shrimp around the bowl of sauce.

Makes at least 10 servings

Pigs in a Blanket

Look, they are NOT sophisticated. They are NOT cool. They are, however, the quintessential party hors d'oeuvres that everyone grew up with. Whenever we have a party, I always insist on these. Pigs in a Blanket may not be chic, but they are tasty and quick, and I guarantee the platter holding them will empty out first.

1 (8-ounce) container refrigerated
crescent dinner rolls
1 (16-ounce) package cocktail hot dogs

Mustard or Mustard-Mayo Sauce
(page 206), for serving

1 • Position a rack in the center of the oven, and preheat the oven to 400°F.

2 • Unwrap the dough and separate each triangle along the perforated marks. Cut each triangle in half and then in half again, making 4 triangles from each piece. You will have 32 triangles total. The average pound of cocktail hot dogs contains about 40 hot dogs, so you will have some left over. Wrap and refrigerate, or freeze for another use.

3 • Wrap each of 32 hot dogs in a mini triangle of the dough and place on a baking sheet. The hot dogs can be covered with plastic wrap and refrigerated for up to 24 hours or frozen. Once frozen (about 2 hours), transfer the hot dogs to an airtight container and freeze for up to 1 month.

4 • Bake for 10 to 12 minutes (1 or 2 minutes longer if frozen), or until the dough turns golden in color and the hot dogs are heated through.

5 • Spoon mustard or Mustard-Mayo Sauce into a small bowl and place it in the center of a serving platter. Arrange the hot dogs around the bowl and serve them hot or warm.

Makes about 32 pieces

Pigs in Down Blankets

Thaw a 10-inch square sheet of frozen puff pastry (half of a 17.3-ounce package) according to package directions, and cut it into 1-inch by 2-inch strips. Wrap each strip around a hot dog. Follow the directions above for storing or baking.

Swedish Meatballs

Mom was always trying to broaden our culinary horizons, while I was just broadening my waistline. One of her girlfriends served Swedish meatballs at a party and Isabel decided to try 'em out on her family.

I don't think that anyone was gonna mistake us for some Scandinavians, but we did a pretty mean yodel. Try these and see how you sound. YODEL-AYYYY-EEEEE-HOOOOOOOOO!!!!

1 pound ground beef	Salt
1 pound sweet "country-style" sausage, loose or removed from casings	Freshly ground pepper
	6 tablespoons all-purpose flour
1 small onion, peeled and minced	About 2 tablespoons canola oil or other vegetable oil, plus more if needed
1 cup homemade bread crumbs (page 141) or store-bought bread crumbs	About 2 tablespoons unsalted butter, plus more if needed
½ cup half-and-half, heavy cream, or evaporated milk	1 cup canned chicken broth
¼ teaspoon ground nutmeg	2 cups sour cream
⅛ teaspoon ground ginger	Sweet paprika

1 • In a large bowl, mix together the beef, sausage, onion, bread crumbs, half-and-half, nutmeg, ginger, 1 teaspoon salt and ½ teaspoon pepper. Roll into 1-inch balls.

2 • Spoon 4 tablespoons of the flour into a shallow bowl, and quickly roll each meatball in it to dust lightly. Shake off any excess flour.

3 • Warm the oil and butter in a large skillet over medium-high heat until the butter begins to foam. Add a dozen or so meatballs and brown them on all sides, about 5 minutes. Remove them from the pan with a slotted spoon and place them in a pot that is large enough to hold all the meatballs and several cups of sauce. Working in batches, and adding more oil and butter to the pan if needed, continue until all of the meatballs are browned.

4 • Reduce the heat under the skillet to medium-low, and sprinkle the remaining 2 tablespoons flour over the bottom. Cook, stirring to scrape up any browned bits from the

bottom of the skillet, and slowly pour in the chicken broth. Adjust the heat to simmer the broth, stirring occasionally, until slightly thickened, 3 to 5 minutes. Stir in the sour cream and season with paprika, salt, and pepper. Simmer for 5 to 8 minutes, until the sauce is the consistency of gravy.

5 • Pour the sauce over the meatballs, and simmer the meatballs for 20 minutes over medium heat. Remove a meatball from the pot and slice in half; the meatball should be browned throughout. If it is still pink, return it to the sauce and cook some more, checking for doneness at 5-minute intervals. The meatballs can be cooled, covered, and refrigerated in the sauce for up to 24 hours. Reheat gently before serving; do not allow the sauce to boil.

6 • Transfer the meatballs to a chafing dish, or to a heatproof dish set on a warming tray, and serve with toothpicks for spearing.

Makes 60 meatballs

Edible Toothpicks

Use thin pretzels as edible toothpicks to spear Swedish Meatballs and other, small party foods. They add salt and crunch and keep you from having to pick up toothpicks during cleanup.

Rumaki

There are reasons that certain cocktail nibbles are still around. They just taste good. There are cave paintings in France of tribes eating rumaki. Some things are just meant to be. Ommmmmm.

1 pound chicken livers, cut into 24 bite-size pieces
¼ cup soy sauce
1 tablespoon brandy
1 tablespoon honey
½ teaspoon ground ginger
12 strips bacon, cut in half
1 (8-ounce) can sliced water chestnuts, drained

1 • Put the chicken livers in a medium bowl. Mix together the soy sauce, brandy, honey, and ginger. Pour over the chicken livers, cover, and refrigerate for at least 30 minutes and up to 2 hours.

2 • Position a rack in the center of the oven and preheat the oven to 400°F.

3 • Drain the chicken livers, pair each with a slice of water chestnut, and wrap with a half-strip of bacon, securing the bundle with a toothpick. (You will have water chestnuts left over; save them, covered and refrigerated, for another use). Place the rumaki on a broiler pan or other rimmed baking pan. The rumaki can be covered and refrigerated for up to 8 hours.

4 • Bake the rumaki until the bacon is crisp, 18 to 20 minutes. Arrange on a warm platter and serve hot or warm.

Makes 24 pieces

VARIATION

Scallop Rumaki

Substitute 2 dozen large sea scallops for the chicken livers.

Chocolate Fondue

Rummage around your parents' kitchen cabinets, attic, or basement and I'm sure you will find a fondue pot. It may even still be in the gift paper it came in. Sure it was big in the late sixties and seventies. But fondue is back, baby, and it's not just cheese anymore. We're talkin' chocolate. Combine this for dessert and a game of Twister and neighbors'll be calling the cops. Now that's a party!!!!

1 pound semisweet chocolate, chopped, or 2¾ cups semisweet chocolate chips
1 cup heavy cream

¼ cup whole milk
2 teaspoons pure vanilla or almond extract

In a double boiler set over simmering water, combine the chocolate, cream, and milk. Stir occasionally until the chocolate is melted and the mixture is smooth. Stir in the vanilla extract. Transfer to a fondue pot, or keep warm in the double boiler.

TO SERVE

1 pint strawberries, hulled
2 bananas, peeled and sliced

2 oranges or 3 tangerines, peeled and separated into sections
1 ripe pear or apple, cored and sliced

Arrange the fruit on a platter and lay fondue forks or bamboo skewers on the side of the platter. Scrape the fondue into a fondue pot, or into a warm bowl set on a warming tray. Bring the fondue to the table. Skewer the fruit and dip it into the warm chocolate.

Makes 10 servings

Super Bowl Party

Let's face it. Given the mediocrity of most Super Bowl games, the only reasons to give or go to a Super Bowl party are the commercials and the chance to get together with friends and eat food you normally wouldn't touch.

We've all thrown or gone to Super Bowl parties that were not so super. I mean, how many variations on a theme can there be? Don't get fancy or try to be cute. The idea of a party like this is to have fun. People expect certain things from a Super Bowl party. They expect the game to stink, and they expect a lot of good food. There's nothing you can do about the game, but you can take care of the food.

The best part about the Super Bowl party is that a lot of the dishes can be made ahead of time. I've included some classics, some twists on classics, and a few you might not have thought of. So, go long, take a hook at the end of the sofa, and enjoy so that you can enjoy yourselves and your guests. Enjoy the game? Well, that's debatable. But how about those commercials?

Nachos

Nachos are a staple of any Super Bowl party and unless you're REALLY bad in the kitchen, or you still live with Mommy, you know how to make these. But, believe it or not, there are those who still use cheese from a jar to make nachos. They are to be pitied, not ridiculed. If you go to such a person's home and are served this abomination, give them a copy of this book. And pray.

4 ounces tortilla chips (about 6 cups)
1 (16-ounce) can refried beans
1 (3-ounce) can jalapeño peppers,
    drained and chopped
1 (2¼-ounce) can sliced black olives,
    drained
6 ounces grated Monterey Jack
    cheese (about 1½ cups)
Toppings of your choice (see opposite)

1 • Position a rack in the center of the oven and preheat the oven to 450°F. Lightly oil a 9 by 13-inch baking dish with sides at least 1½ inches high.

2 • Using a table knife, put a spoonful of refried beans on each tortilla chip. Place the chips in the prepared baking dish. Sprinkle with the jalapeños and olives and top with the cheese. The dish can be covered and refrigerated for up to 4 hours.

3 • Bake until the cheese is melted and bubbling, about 10 minutes. Serve right from the baking dish, with an assortment of toppings, if desired.

Makes 8 servings

VARIATION

Meaty Nachos

Before topping with cheese, sprinkle the chips with ½ pound ground beef, ground turkey or loose sausage, cooked and drained.

Toppings

After baking, garnish with any of the following:

- *Chopped scallions*
- *Chopped cilantro leaves*
- *Diced ripe avocado*
- *Green salsa, homemade (page 98) or store-bought*
- *Red salsa, homemade (page 196) or store-bought*
- *Sour cream*

Spicy Chicken Wings

I went to school at the State University of New York at Oswego, or Oswego State as I like to call it. We were just up the road from Buffalo. For the longest time, I thought Buffalo was named after the wings. My college roommate, Dave Prohaska took me home to visit one weekend. He lived in North Tonowanda, New York, and it was there that I had my first taste of Buffalo wings. Nirvana. There's a game on? Who cares? MORE WINGS!!

¼ cup hot sauce
¼ cup honey
¼ cup unsalted butter, melted
4 teaspoons chili powder

1 teaspoon salt
1 (5 pound) bag frozen chicken wings
    or drumettes, thawed
Blue Cheese Dressing (page 53)

1 • In a small bowl, whisk together the hot sauce, honey, butter, chili powder, and salt. Put the chicken pieces in a shallow pan and pour the marinade on top. Turn to coat. The chicken should be just coated, not swimming in marinade. Cover the chicken with plastic wrap and refrigerate for at least 2 hours and up to 12 hours.

2 • Position a rack in the middle of the oven and preheat the oven to 375°F. Using heavy-duty aluminum foil, line two 9 by 13-inch baking dishes. Divide the chicken between the dishes in a single layer.

3 • Bake until the wings begin to crisp, about 1 hour and 15 minutes. These are best served shortly after baking, but they can be refrigerated, covered, for up to 24 hours. Serve cold, or reheat in a foil-covered baking dish in a preheated 400°F oven for 10 to 15 minutes.

4 • Pour the Blue Cheese Dressing into a bowl, place the bowl in the center of a platter, and arrange the wings around the bowl.

Makes 10 servings

Asian Wings

Substitute a mixture of ½ cup apricot jam, ¼ cup soy sauce, 4 teaspoons rice vinegar, and 2 teaspoons sesame oil for the marinade. Serve hot, and omit the Blue Cheese Dressing.

Spicy Party Mix

What's a party without party mix? I guarantee this one will taste better than the bagged variety you get off the shelf, and because it doesn't have a lot of unpronounceable additives in it, it's better for you, too.

8 tablespoons (1 stick) unsalted butter, melted
3 tablespoons hot sauce
1 tablespoon Worcestershire sauce
2 cups O-shaped oat cereal
2 cups toasted corn cereal squares

2 cups bite-size shredded wheat cereal
2 cups mixed nuts, preferably lightly salted
1 cup pretzel nuggets or thin pretzel sticks
1 cup bite-size cheese crackers

1 • Position a rack in the center of the oven and preheat the oven to 250°F. Lightly butter a 9 by 13-inch baking dish with sides at least 1½ inches high.

2 • Combine the butter, hot sauce, and Worcestershire sauce. Set aside.

3 • Stir together the cereals, nuts, pretzels, and crackers in the prepared dish. Pour the butter mixture on top. Toss to coat well.

4 • Bake the mix for 1 hour, stirring every 15 minutes, until lightly browned and crisped. Remove the baking dish from the oven and place it on a wire rack to cool thoroughly.

5 • Serve the mix immediately or store in an airtight container for up to 1 week.

Makes 10 cups, or at least 20 servings

Meaty Chili

Debate about chili is almost as hot as the debate over which is better, dry ribs or wet. Should chili have beans? Should you use ground beef? Here's the deal: I have a cookbook, you don't. This is my version: beans all the way—three kinds, in fact—along with chunks of beef and spicy Italian sausage. When you get a cookbook, you'll put your version in it. Doesn't mean I got a franchise on chili, so don't get your knickers in a twist over my version . . . we clear?

1 pound hot Italian sausage, removed from casings
2 pounds chuck steak, cut into 1½-inch cubes
Salt
Freshly ground pepper
Canola or other vegetable oil, if needed
2 large onions, peeled and cut into ½-inch pieces
12 cloves garlic, peeled and finely chopped
1 tablespoon ground cumin
1 tablespoon sweet paprika
1 tablespoon chili powder
1 (28-ounce) can crushed tomatoes
1 (15½-ounce) can pinto beans, rinsed and drained
1 (15½-ounce) can Great Northern beans, rinsed and drained
1 (15½-ounce) can dark red kidney beans, rinsed and drained
Corn and Cheese Muffins (page 137), for serving, optional
Chopped scallions, sour cream, and grated cheddar or Monterey Jack cheese for serving, optional

1 • Cook the sausage in a large pot over medium heat, stirring occasionally, until well browned, 12 to 15 minutes. Using a slotted spoon, transfer the sausage to a plate and set aside.

2 • Season the chuck steak with salt and pepper and add to the pot. Cook, turning, until the meat is browned on all sides, 7 to 10 minutes. Using a slotted spoon, add the meat to the sausage and set aside.

3 • Drain all but about 2 tablespoons of fat from the pot. (If there is not enough fat, add the oil as needed.) Add the onions and garlic and cook over medium heat, stirring, until soft-

ened but not browned, about 5 minutes. Add the cumin, paprika, and chili powder and stir for 1 minute. Add the tomatoes and the cooked sausage and beef and stir well. Cook over low heat, with the pot partially covered, for 1½ to 2 hours, or until the beef is tender. Add the beans and cook for 30 minutes more. The chili can be cooled, covered, and refrigerated for up to 2 days or frozen, well wrapped, for up to 1 month (thaw before proceeding). Reheat gently before serving.

4 • Serve hot over split corn muffins with chopped scallions, sour cream, and grated cheese, if desired.

Makes 8 servings

Corn and Cheese Muffins

One inviolable rule when it comes to chili: You gotta have some sort of corn bread. When it's a party, I like muffins over bread. They're neater and easier to hold. Plus the leftover muffins can be frozen nicely. (As if there'll be any.)

1/3 cup extra-virgin olive oil
1/2 medium onion, peeled and finely
    chopped
1¼ cups all-purpose flour
1¼ cups cornmeal
1 tablespoon baking powder
1 teaspoon salt

1 cup whole milk or evaporated milk
2 large eggs
3 tablespoons honey
1 cup fresh or frozen and thawed corn
    kernels
2 ounces grated cheddar cheese
    (½ cup)

1 • Position a rack in the center of the oven and preheat the oven to 375°F. Lightly butter a standard (2½-inch) or large (3½-inch) muffin tin.

2 • Warm the oil in a small skillet over medium heat. Add the onion and cook, stirring, until softened and just beginning to brown, about 8 minutes. Set aside to cool.

3 • In a large bowl, whisk or stir together the flour, cornmeal, baking powder, and salt.

4 • In a smaller bowl, whisk together the milk, eggs, and honey. Add the liquid to the dry ingredients, stirring just until combined. Stir in the reserved onion, corn, and cheddar.

5 • Spoon about 1/3 cup batter into the standard muffin tins, or 2/3 cup into the large tins. Bake for 18 to 20 minutes for standard muffins, or 20 to 25 minutes for large. A knife inserted into the center of a muffin should come out clean.

6 • Remove the muffins from the tins and place them on a wire rack to cool, at least partially. Serve warm or at room temperature.

7 • The muffins are best served shortly after they are made, but can be cooled and frozen, well wrapped, for up to 1 month. Thaw and reheat—wrapped in aluminum foil—in a preheated 350°F oven for about 10 minutes.

Makes twelve standard 2½-inch muffins or six large 3½-inch muffins

NOTE: You can also bake this recipe in a buttered 8-inch square baking pan. Allow 25 to 30 minutes for baking; cool and cut into 3-inch squares or wrap well and freeze unsliced. Thaw, cut into squares, and reheat as directed for about 8 minutes.

Muffuletta

Okay, forget about your typical six-foot sub. Let's try something a little more exotic. Howzabout a muffuletta?

What's a muffuletta? Sounds like an Italian sports car, doesn't it? Well, you're half right. It started in New Orleans, born in the French Quarter's Italian markets as a whole meal in a sandwich for the local sailors.

Generally a large, round sandwich that features a ton of different meats and cheeses, it's perfect for feeding any Super Bowl crowd, I guar-an-teeee!

1 cup chopped pitted green olives with pimientos
1 cup chopped pitted imported black olives, such as Kalamata
1/2 cup extra-virgin olive oil
1/2 cup chopped parsley leaves
2 teaspoons chopped basil leaves, or 1 teaspoon dried basil
2 teaspoons chopped oregano leaves, or 1 teaspoon dried oregano
1/2 teaspoon hot red pepper flakes
2 cloves garlic, peeled and finely chopped

1 large round loaf (at least 8 inches in diameter) Italian or French bread
4 ounces thinly sliced mortadella or ham
4 ounces thinly sliced Genoa salami, sopressata, or other hard salami
4 ounces thinly sliced provolone cheese
2 medium tomatoes, stemmed, cored, and thinly sliced
1 cup watercress, arugula, or other salad greens

1 • At least 12 hours—and up to 36 hours—before you plan to serve the sandwich, mix together the green and black olives, olive oil, parsley, basil, oregano, red pepper flakes, and garlic in a bowl. Cover and refrigerate.

2 • Split the bread in half and remove a good bit of the soft bread inside each half, to create a well. (You can use the excess bread to make fresh bread crumbs—see page 141—or reserve it for another use.) Spread half of the olive mixture on the bottom half of the bread. In layers, add the mortadella, salami, provolone, tomatoes, and greens. Top with the remaining olive mixture, cover with the other half of the bread, and wrap tightly in several layers of plastic wrap. Put the sandwich on a large plate, and cover it with

another plate. Place several pounds of heavy weights on the top plate—canned foods work well, as do heavy cookbooks. Let sit at room temperature for at least 30 minutes and up to 2 hours.

3 • To serve, unwrap the muffuletta and cut into 6 wedges.

Makes 6 servings

Mac and Cheese

My mother makes the world's greatest macaroni and cheese. That's it, case closed, let's move on. Your mom probably makes the world's greatest mac 'n cheese. Case closed, let's move on. Now it's time for you to make the greatest mac 'n cheese. You owe it to your friends. Case closed, let's move on.

1 pound elbow macaroni
1 quart whole milk or half-and-half
5 tablespoons unsalted butter
¼ cup all-purpose flour
1¼ pounds grated cheddar cheese,
*   or a combination of cheddar and*
*   American cheese (5 cups)*

1 tablespoon Dijon mustard
Salt
Freshly ground pepper
⅔ cup homemade bread crumbs
*   (see opposite) or store-bought*
*   bread crumbs*

1 • Position a rack in the center of the oven and preheat the oven to 375°F.

2 • Butter a 3½-quart baking dish or a 9 by 13-inch baking dish with sides at least 1½ inches high.

3 • Bring a large pot of salted water to a boil, add the macaroni and cook according to package directions until al dente (cooked but still firm). Drain well and place in the prepared baking dish.

4 • Warm the milk in a small saucepan over medium heat.

5 • Melt 4 tablespoons of the butter in a large saucepan over medium-low heat. Sprinkle in the flour and cook, whisking constantly, until the mixture is thick and smooth, about 3 minutes. Gradually add the warm milk, still whisking, to make a smooth sauce. Increase the heat to medium and simmer, stirring, until smooth and thick, about 5 minutes.

6 • Remove the pot from the heat, add the cheese, and stir until melted. Stir in the mustard and season with salt and pepper. Pour the sauce over the macaroni in the baking dish and stir to combine. The dish can be covered and refrigerated for up to 24 hours (bring to room temperature before proceeding).

7 • Sprinkle the macaroni with the bread crumbs. Cut the remaining tablespoon of butter into small pieces and scatter it over the top.

8 • Bake until the bread crumbs begin to brown, about 35 minutes. Let stand for 10 minutes before serving, or cool, cover, and freeze for up to 1 month (thaw, then reheat, covered, in a 325°F oven for about 20 minutes before serving).

Makes 8 servings

VARIATION

Spicy Mac and Cheese

Reduce the amount of milk to 3 cups and add 2 cups drained, chunky salsa when you add the cheese sauce.

TO MAKE BREAD CRUMBS: Use a food processor or a blender to turn slices of day-old white, French, or Italian bread into bread crumbs. One slice of white bread will make about 1/3 cup of crumbs. Spread the crumbs on a rimmed baking sheet and dry them in a preheated 275°F oven for 20 to 30 minutes, stirring occasionally. Remove from the oven and let cool completely. Store in an airtight container for up to 1 week.

Overnight Salad

When you're planning for a Super Bowl party, you don't want it to look like you've been planning for a Super Bowl party. It should look off the cuff and sort of spontaneous . . . like a kegger with class. Here's a salad that you can actually make the night before, which will give you more time on Super Bowl Sunday to blow up the inflatable furniture with your team's logo on it.

½ medium head iceberg lettuce
1 medium head romaine lettuce
1 (3.8-ounce) can sliced black olives, drained (about 1 cup)
4 tablespoons cider vinegar
Salt
Freshly ground pepper

1 red bell pepper, stemmed, seeded, and chopped
4 medium carrots, peeled and grated
½ large red onion, peeled and cut into thin rings
1½ cups mayonnaise
8 ounces grated cheddar cheese (2 cups)

1 • With a sharp knife, core the iceberg lettuce. Place the lettuce, cut side down, on a cutting board and chop into bite-size pieces. Separate the romaine leaves, stack them on the cutting board and chop them into bite-size pieces. Wash all the lettuce and spin dry. You should have about 10 cups of chopped lettuce.

2 • Place the olives in the bottom of a 4-quart glass bowl, cover with a quarter of the lettuce, sprinkle with 1 tablespoon vinegar, and season with salt and pepper. Top with a layer of bell pepper. Repeat with two more layers, using the remaining lettuce (sprinkling each layer with a tablespoon of vinegar and salt and pepper), and using the carrots and then the onion in place of the red pepper. You will finish with a layer of lettuce.

3 • Spoon the mayonnaise over the top and smooth it with a flat spatula or a butter knife. Sprinkle the grated cheese on top. Cover with plastic wrap and refrigerate for at least 12 hours and up to 24 hours.

4 • Just before serving, toss the salad, digging deep to the bottom of the bowl to mix together all of the ingredients.

Makes 10 servings

Texas Sheet Cake

In keeping with the casualness of our Super Bowl party, you cannot have a fancy schmancy dessert. But you need something that will feed a crowd. This cake recipe is just the ticket. Plop a gallon of good-quality vanilla ice cream next to it and your partygoers will drench you in neon sports drink and hoist you on their shoulders.

FOR THE CAKE

8 tablespoons (1 stick) unsalted
    butter, softened (page 25)
1½ cups sugar
2 large eggs
½ cup water
1 tablespoon pure vanilla extract
2 cups all-purpose flour

½ teaspoon salt
½ teaspoon baking soda
½ teaspoon baking powder
1 cup buttermilk
4 ounces semisweet chocolate or
    ⅔ cup semisweet chocolate
    chips, melted (page 42)

1 • Position a rack in the center of the oven and preheat the oven to 350°F. Lightly butter a 9 by 13-inch baking pan with sides at least 1½ inches high.

2 • Using an electric mixer or mixing by hand, beat the butter and sugar together until fluffy, 3 to 5 minutes. Add the eggs, water, and vanilla and beat until well combined. In a small bowl, stir together the flour, salt, baking soda, and baking powder. Gradually stir the dry ingredients into the butter mixture, alternating with the buttermilk, to make a smooth batter. Do not overmix. Pour in the melted chocolate and mix just until the batter is a uniform color.

3 • Pour into the prepared pan and bake for 20 to 25 minutes, or until a knife inserted in the center comes out clean. Remove from the oven, place on a wire rack, and cool partially.

FOR THE FROSTING

2 cups confectioners' sugar
4 tablespoons (½ stick) unsalted
   butter, softened (page 25)
½ teaspoon pure vanilla extract
¼ cup heavy cream or half-and-half

Pinch of salt
2 ounces semisweet chocolate or
   ⅓ cup semisweet chocolate chips,
   melted (page 42)

1 • Using an electric mixer or mixing by hand, beat the sugar, butter, and vanilla until smooth. Add the cream and salt and mix again. Stir in the chocolate until the frosting is a uniform color. The icing will be slightly runny; spoon it over the warm cake, smoothing with a table knife or offset spatula. As the cake cools, the icing will set.

2 • Once the icing is set, the cake can be covered and stored at room temperature for up to 3 days or frozen, well wrapped, for up to 6 weeks (thaw before slicing).

3 • Serve from the pan, cutting the cake into twelve 3-inch squares.

Makes 12 servings

Groundhog Day
Weatherman's Meal

I know it's not a REAL holiday, but I'm a weatherman. I would be remiss if I didn't include Groundhog Day. Look, this holiday actually annoys me. I'm the king of weather for 364 days a year. But for one day, February 2nd, a nasty, burrow-making rodent gets held up in front of a battery of TV lights and declared the weather god. "Punxsutawney Phil has seen his shadow . . . six more weeks of winter" is the usual declaration. Heck, in all those lights, of course he's gonna see his shadow. Ray Charles could see his shadow in those conditions.

Anyway, I'm going with some recipes that bring the cold weather and warmer weather seasons together. I hope that's okay with . . . Phillllll.

Chilled Pea Soup

In case the weather turns warm because Phil didn't see his shadow, we present this lovely, chilled celebration-of-spring soup.

3 cups canned vegetable or chicken broth
2 shallots, peeled and chopped
2 sprigs rosemary
1½ pounds frozen peas, preferably
    "petits pois" or tiny peas

1½ cups light cream or whole milk
1 small cucumber, peeled, seeded, and
    grated (about ¾ cup)
Salt
Freshly ground pepper

1 • Combine the broth, shallots, and rosemary in a saucepan and bring to a boil. Reduce the heat, cover, and simmer for 5 minutes. Add the peas and cook until just tender but still bright green, 3 to 4 minutes. Discard the rosemary. Pour the soup into a blender or food processor and puree until smooth. Refrigerate until cool, about 1 hour.

2 • Stir in the cream and cucumber and season with salt and pepper. Cover and refrigerate until quite cold, at least 3 hours and up to 24 hours.

3 • To serve, ladle into 8 chilled bowls.

Makes about 10 cups, or 8 servings

Hot Split Pea Soup

If there's a woolly mammoth on your front lawn, odds are things aren't warming up anytime soon. Go with this pea soup to get you through those last weeks of winter.

2 tablespoons canola oil, or other
    vegetable oil
2 medium onions, peeled and cut into
    ¼-inch pieces
2 stalks celery, trimmed and cut into
    ¼-inch pieces
2 large carrots, peeled and cut into
    ¼-inch pieces
1 tablespoon thyme leaves, or
    1 teaspoon dried thyme
1½ pounds split peas, picked over,
    rinsed, and drained (3½ cups)

10 cups canned chicken or vegetable
    broth or water
1 sprig rosemary
1 smoked ham hock or ham bone left
    over from Glazed Baked Ham
    (page 180), optional
Salt
Freshly ground pepper
Homemade croutons (page 69),
    or store-bought croutons, for
    serving

1 • Warm the oil in a large pot over medium-high heat. Add the onions, celery, carrots, and thyme and cook, stirring, for 5 minutes. Add the peas, broth, rosemary, and ham hock, if using.

2 • Lower the heat, cover the pot, and simmer for 1½ to 2 hours, until the peas are very tender. Transfer the ham hock to a cutting board and slice any meat off the bone. Discard the bone, finely chop the meat, and set aside.

3 • Working in batches, puree the soup in a food processor or blender until quite smooth. Return the pureed soup to the pot, season with salt and pepper, and add the meat. The soup can be cooled, covered, and refrigerated for up to 2 days or frozen, well wrapped, for up to 1 month (thaw, then reheat gently).

4 • Serve hot, ladling into 10 warm bowls and sprinkling croutons on each serving.

Makes 12 cups, or 8 servings

Pasta Primavera

This is a great pasta dish that uses the veggies of spring to signal that our long hibernation is over and it's time to come out of our burrow. Isn't that poetic? As if living underground for three months and an incredible case of morning mouth would be poetic? I'm not bitter about this groundhog thing. I'm really not!

Florets from 1 bunch broccoli, cut into bite-size pieces (about 5 cups)
1 pound asparagus, trimmed and cut into 1½-inch pieces
1 pound green beans, trimmed and cut into 1½-inch pieces
¼ cup extra-virgin olive oil
1 pound button mushrooms, wiped clean and sliced
4 cloves garlic, peeled and finely chopped
Salt

6 medium tomatoes (about 2 pounds), stemmed, cored, seeded, and diced
½ cup chopped parsley leaves
2 pounds spaghetti or linguini
6 tablespoons (¾ stick) unsalted butter
2 cups half-and-half or heavy cream
8 ounces freshly grated Parmesan cheese (2 cups), plus extra for serving
Freshly ground pepper

1 • Bring a large pot of salted water to a boil. Add the broccoli, asparagus, and green beans and cook until just tender but still very green, about 4 minutes. Using a slotted spoon, transfer the vegetables to a colander; reserve the pot of water. Rinse the vegetables under cold water to stop the cooking, then drain and set aside for up to 4 hours, or cool, cover, and refrigerate for up to 1 day.

2 • Warm the oil in a medium saucepan over medium heat. Add the mushrooms and garlic and sprinkle with salt. Cover and cook, stirring occasionally, for about 10 minutes, until the mushrooms begin to give up some liquid. Add the tomatoes, stir, and cook, uncovered, for about 5 more minutes. Stir in the parsley. Remove the mixture from the heat and set aside for up to 4 hours, or cool, cover, and refrigerate for up to 1 day.

3 • Bring the reserved pot of water back to a full boil and add the pasta. Cook according to package directions until al dente (cooked but still firm). Drain well.

4 • In a pot large enough to hold all of the ingredients, melt the butter over medium heat. Add the half-and-half and Parmesan and stir constantly until heated through and smooth, 3 to 5 minutes. Add the pasta and toss quickly to coat. Add the vegetables and the mushroom-tomato mixture and stir over low heat until everything is heated through, 3 to 5 minutes. Season with salt and pepper.

5 • Serve immediately, spooning the pasta into warm, shallow bowls, and sprinkling each serving with additional Parmesan cheese.

Makes 8 servings

Pot Roast with Pennsylvania Dutch Noodles

If winter is still hanging on, no one knows better about keeping warm than Punxsutawney Phil's neighbors, the Pennsylvania Dutch. I remember eating at a Pennsylvania Dutch restaurant when we were coming home on a bus trip from Washington, D.C., when I was about eight. I'd never seen so much food on one plate in my life. I had the pot roast. Good Lord. Did they know I was eight and not a forty-three-year-old coal miner? I guess you eat when you can, fill up, and hunker down. So in that spirit, I offer this dish.

3 pounds chuck or rump roast
2 cloves garlic, peeled and cut into slivers
Salt
Freshly ground pepper
3 tablespoons canola oil, or other vegetable oil
1 medium onion, peeled and thinly sliced
1 stalk celery, trimmed and cut into ½-inch pieces

5 large carrots, peeled
3 tablespoons tomato paste
1 cup canned beef broth, or more if needed
1 cup red wine, or more if needed
2 bay leaves
1 tablespoon chopped thyme leaves, or 1 teaspoon dried thyme
1 pound pearl onions, peeled
1½ pounds extra-wide egg noodles
2 tablespoons all-purpose flour

1 • Rinse the meat under cold running water and pat it dry with paper towels. Using a small, sharp knife, cut a dozen small slits in the meat and tuck the garlic slivers into the slits. Season the roast with salt and pepper.

2 • Warm the oil in a large pot over medium-high heat. When quite hot, add the meat to the pan and brown well on all sides, turning as needed, 7 to 10 minutes. Remove the meat from the pot and set aside.

3 • Scatter the sliced onion and celery in the pot. Cut 1 of the carrots into ½-inch rounds and add to the pot. Cook the vegetables for five minutes, stirring. Stir in the tomato paste. Return the meat to the pot and add the broth, wine, bay leaves, and thyme.

Reduce the heat to low, cover the pot, and cook barely at a simmer until the meat is very tender, 2 to 2½ hours, turning the meat every 45 minutes or so. If the liquid in the pot seems low, add more broth or wine. (If the heat is low enough, you should not need to add more liquid.)

4 • Transfer the meat to a cutting board and strain the cooking liquid, discarding the cooked vegetables. Return the meat and the cooking liquid to the pot.

5 • Cut the remaining 4 carrots into 1-inch chunks and add to the pot along with the pearl onions. Simmer, covered, over low heat until the vegetables are tender, about 20 minutes. The dish can be cooled, covered, and refrigerated for up to 2 days or frozen, well wrapped, for up to 2 months (thaw and reheat gently before proceeding).

6 • Bring a large pot of salted water to a boil, add the noodles, and cook according to package directions until al dente (cooked but still firm). Drain well, cover to keep warm, and set aside.

7 • Transfer the meat to a cutting board and the vegetables to a warm platter. Cover both loosely with aluminum foil to keep warm. In a small bowl, mix the flour with 2 tablespoons of the cooking liquid and stir well. Add this paste to the cooking liquid in the pot and heat gently, stirring occasionally, for about 5 minutes, until the sauce thickens. Cut the meat into ½-inch slices and arrange on the platter surrounded by the vegetables. Pour the sauce on top.

8 • To serve, spoon noodles into warm, shallow bowls and top with a serving of meat, vegetables, and gravy.

Makes 8 servings

Sunshine Cake

Work with me here. It's a weather-related holiday. I call it sunshine cake because of the yellow hue the eggs give the batter and the lemony taste. Lemons are yellow. The sun is yellow. By the associative property (sixth grade math) this is a Sunshine Cake . . . TA DAAAAAA!

7 large eggs, at room temperature
1¼ cups confectioners' sugar
1 tablespoon finely grated lemon zest
    (from 1 to 2 lemons)
2 tablespoons lemon juice (from 1 lemon)

½ teaspoon pure vanilla extract
1 teaspoon cream of tartar
1 cup all-purpose flour
¼ teaspoon salt

1 • Position a rack in the center of the oven and preheat the oven to 325°F. Line the bottom of a 9-inch, preferably springform, tube pan with parchment paper.

2 • Separate the eggs. In a large bowl, whisk together the egg yolks, 1 cup of the sugar, the lemon zest, lemon juice, and vanilla. Continue whisking until very thick, about 3 minutes. Set aside.

3 • In a large, very clean bowl (any trace of grease will keep the whites from whipping to their fullest volume), whip the egg whites and cream of tartar with an electric mixer on medium-high speed or a wire whisk until they hold soft peaks. Gradually add the remaining ¼ cup sugar, whipping constantly until medium peaks form. Do not overbeat.

4 • Sprinkle the flour and salt over the yolk mixture and, using a rubber spatula, gently fold it in. Then gently fold in the whites, mixing until just combined.

5 • Spoon the batter into the prepared pan and bake for about 50 minutes, or until a knife inserted in the center comes out clean.

6 • Remove the cake from the oven, invert the pan on a wire rack, and let cool completely. Turn the pan right side up and run a knife around the side of the pan and around the tube. If using a regular tube pan, invert the cake again, remove the pan, peel off the paper, and turn the cake upright on the rack. If using a springform pan, simply remove the sides;

you can remove the cake entirely, if desired, or you can let it sit on the bottom part of the pan for serving. The cake can be stored, well wrapped, at room temperature for up to 3 days or frozen for up to 1 week (thaw at room temperature before serving).

7 • Slice the cake with a serrated knife and serve plain or with berries and whipped cream, if desired.

Makes one 9-inch tube cake, or about 10 servings

Mud Pie

If it won't be getting sunny anytime soon, it will definitely be getting muddy. Help winter go out in style with this chocolaty, candy-and-nut-studded, delicious mess.

FOR THE CRUST

1 store-bought (9-inch) graham
    cracker or chocolate cookie crust
or
1½ cups chocolate wafer crumbs
    (25 to 30 wafers)

6 tablespoons (¾ stick) unsalted
    butter, melted

1 • Position a rack in the center of the oven. Preheat the oven to 350°F.

2 • In a medium bowl, mix together the cookie crumbs and melted butter. Press into a 9-inch pie plate. Bake until the crust begins to puff up, about 8 minutes. Remove from the oven and place on a wire rack to cool. The crust must be thoroughly cooled before you proceed.

FOR THE FILLING

1 cup (½ pint) chocolate ice cream,
    slightly softened (see opposite)
½ cup chopped pecans, toasted
    (page 23)

½ cup milk chocolate toffee candy bits
    (available in the baking aisle of the
    supermarket) or 2 (1.4-ounce) milk
    chocolate toffee bars, crushed, or
    ½ cup mini chocolate chips
1 cup (½ pint) coffee ice cream,
    slightly softened (see opposite)

Spoon the chocolate ice cream into the cooled crust. Using a flat metal spatula or a butter knife, smooth the top of the ice cream so that it is even. Sprinkle the pecans and candy bits on top. Spoon the coffee ice cream on top, smoothing to even it. Wrap in plastic wrap and freeze for at least 2 hours or up to 2 weeks.

FOR THE CHOCOLATE SAUCE

1 cup store-bought chocolate sauce or fudge sauce, warmed
or
6 ounces semisweet chocolate or 1 cup semisweet chocolate chips, melted (page 42)

2 tablespoons unsalted butter, melted
½ cup heavy cream, at room temperature

1 • Stir together the chocolate and butter. Slowly stir in the cream, mixing until very smooth. The sauce can be cooled and refrigerated in a heatproof jar for up to 1 week.

2 • If the sauce was refrigerated, reheat the jar of sauce in a saucepan of simmering water, stirring occasionally, until the sauce is heated through, or microwave (make sure to remove any metal lids). Warm at half power for about 2 minutes, stirring halfway through.

3 • Unwrap the pie and cut it into 8 slices with a knife that has been dipped in hot water, redipping before cutting each additional slice. Place each slice on a plate and drizzle with warm chocolate sauce. Top with a dollop of whipped cream, if desired.

Makes one 9-inch pie, or 8 servings

TO SOFTEN ICE CREAM: Warm it in the microwave oven on high for about 15 seconds, or transfer it from the freezer to the refrigerator about 30 minutes before serving.

Valentine's Day Dinner for Two

This is the holiday of Love. So all of the dishes in this chapter are for two. But if you and your sweetie have a healthy appetite, double 'em. I think it's more romantic to stay in and cook a meal for your sweetie than to go out to a fancy restaurant like everyone else. Plus the cash you save can be plowed right into a nicer gift. Win-Win!!

Is Valentine's Day a real holiday? Maybe not in the true sense, but try blowing it off, fellas. I don't think the "It's not a real holiday, Honey" defense is gonna cut it. So suck it up and get into that kitchen. Do it for Looooove! Think of yourself as Pepe LePew, the amorous skunk from the Sunday morning cartoons.

Then drop the kids at the grandparents, put a little Barry White on the stereo, turn down the lights, and . . . well, I don't think you need a cookbook to tell you what to do next.

Pink Lady

Gotta start with a romantic beverage . . . and no, that's not a pair of long-necks. This is something a little more sophisticated. Playful and subtle with a nice pale pink color in honor of the day. If you're a woman making this, we can rename it the Blushing Boy.

Ice cubes or cracked ice, for chilling
    glasses and for serving
6 tablespoons gin or vodka (3 ounces)
3 tablespoons Cointreau or Triple Sec
    (1½ ounces)

¼ cup lemon juice (from 1 to 2 lemons)
1 tablespoon grenadine
About 1 teaspoon sugar
2 thin strips lemon peel, removed with
    a vegetable peeler, for serving

1 • Chill 2 martini glasses by filling them with ice, and letting them sit as you prepare the drinks.

2 • In a cocktail shaker, combine the gin, Cointreau, lemon juice, grenadine, and sugar. Add ice and shake to mix. (If you don't have a cocktail shaker, use a jar with a lid.) Taste and add more sugar, if needed.

3 • Drain any melted ice from the prepared glasses and top off the glasses with more ice, if needed. Pour the drink—straining out the ice in the shaker—into the glasses. Garnish each glass with a twist of lemon peel and serve.

Makes 2 servings

Smoked Salmon Hors d'Oeuvre

Who doesn't like salmon? And this is a great starter that doesn't take a lot of time, allowing you to concentrate on the rest of the meal and matters of . . . loooooove.

---

6 tablespoons whipped cream cheese
2 teaspoons bottled grated white
    horseradish
½ teaspoon freshly ground pepper

8 slices cucumber (see note), ¼ inch
    thick
2 ounces thinly sliced smoked salmon,
    cut into 8 strips
1 teaspoon capers, drained

---

1 • In a small bowl, mix together the cream cheese, horseradish, and pepper with a fork until well combined.

2 • Spread each cucumber slice with a scant tablespoon of the cream cheese mixture. Wind a salmon strip into a circle and place it on top of the cream cheese. Drop a few capers into the middle of the circle. Serve at once, or cover and refrigerate for up to 4 hours.

Makes 8 pieces, or 2 servings

NOTE: You can peel the cucumber before slicing or leave it unpeeled. Or, to make a decorative edge, run the tines of the fork down the sides of the unpeeled cucumber before slicing.

Herbed Stuffed Mushrooms

Y'know . . . you don't have to be Fellini to love this dish. The roundness of the mushrooms, the aroma of the toasted nuts, the softness of the goat cheese . . . pardon me . . . I think I have the vapors. Excuse me while I recline on the divan.

8 large white mushrooms, about
    2 inches in diameter
3 tablespoons soft, fresh goat cheese
3 tablespoons chopped parsley leaves
1 tablespoon finely chopped shallot or
    onion

1 clove garlic, peeled and finely
    chopped
1 tablespoon pine nuts or walnuts,
    toasted (page 23)
4 tablespoons extra-virgin olive oil
Salt
Freshly ground pepper

1 • Wipe the mushrooms well with a damp paper towel. Remove the stems and set them aside. Using a small spoon, scoop out and discard the dark gills to increase the bowllike area of the mushroom.

2 • Finely chop enough of the stems to make ⅓ cup; discard the rest. Put the chopped stems in a bowl with the goat cheese, parsley, shallot, garlic, nuts, and 2 tablespoons of the olive oil. Season generously with salt and pepper and mix well.

3 • Transfer the mushrooms to a flat work surface and, using a small spoon, fill each cap with stuffing. The mushrooms can be covered and refrigerated for up to 24 hours (return to room temperature before proceeding).

4 • Preheat the broiler with the rack set 5 to 6 inches from the heat source. Pour the remaining 2 tablespoons oil into an 8-inch square baking dish with sides at least 1½ inches high. Put the baking dish, with the oil, under the broiler for 2 minutes to heat.

5 • Transfer the stuffed mushrooms, stuffed side up, to the preheated baking dish and broil until the stuffing starts to bubble and brown, 3 to 4 minutes.

6 • Serve immediately.

Makes 8 pieces, or 2 servings

Filet Mignon

What better way to say "I love you" than with a couple of pieces of expensive, tender, deeeee-licious beef? One ingredient, the RED wine, is perfect for Valentine's Day. Of course, you could omit the filet, olive oil, salt, pepper, shallot, and garlic and just go with the red wine. Your choice.

---

2 tablespoon extra-virgin olive oil
2 pieces filet mignon (8 ounces each)
Coarse salt
Freshly ground pepper

½ cup red wine
1 shallot, peeled and finely chopped
1 clove garlic, peeled and finely chopped

---

1 • Position a rack in the center of the oven and preheat the oven to 450°F.

2 • Warm the oil in a medium, ovenproof skillet over high heat. Season the steaks with salt and pepper. When the oil is very hot, add the meat to the pan, and brown on both sides, about 5 minutes total.

3 • Transfer the skillet to the oven and roast until an instant-read thermometer inserted in the center of each piece of meat registers at least 145°F for medium-rare, 8 to 10 minutes.

4 • Remove the steaks from the skillet and transfer them to a platter. Cover the meat with aluminum foil to keep warm. Place the skillet over medium heat and add the wine, shallot, and garlic. Simmer for about 3 minutes, stirring constantly. Remove from the heat and stir in any meat juices that have collected on the platter.

5 • Serve the steaks immediately, drizzled with the pan juices.

Makes 2 servings

NOTE: The filet mignon roasts at the same temperature as the Oven Fries (page 162), so if you are making them together, just pop the steaks in the oven when the potatoes have about 10 minutes left to roast.

Oven Fries

It's like soup and sandwich, Laurel and Hardy, Democrats and losing. If you're gonna have steak, you have to have fries. But these fries aren't your everyday fries. They're a little heart healthier. And on Valentine's Day, we have to think of your heart.

3 tablespoons extra-virgin olive oil
1 large or 2 medium russet potatoes
    (about 1 pound), scrubbed but
    not peeled

½ teaspoon coarse salt

1 • Position a rack in the center of the oven and preheat the oven to 450°F. Line a plate with paper towels.

2 • Pour the oil into a 9 by 13-inch baking dish with sides at least 1½ inches high. Put the dish in the oven until the oil is very hot, about 5 minutes.

3 • While the oil is heating, cut the potatoes lengthwise into ½-inch slices, and then cut the slices into ¼-inch strips. Carefully place the strips into the pan (the oil may splatter) and generously sprinkle them with salt.

4 • Bake the potatoes for 40 to 50 minutes, turning halfway through, until they are brown and beginning to crisp. Remove from the oven and transfer the potatoes to the prepared plate to drain briefly. Serve hot.

Makes 2 servings

Wilted Spinach

I threw in the spinach in honor of one of the great romantic figures of all time . . . Popeye. I mean, granted, Popeye was no looker, but he followed his heart to Olive Oyl. WOW! Now that's love. But he had stamina . . . why? Because he eats his spinach. Ack . . . Ack Ack Ack!

---

8 cups lightly packed spinach, prefer-
ably baby spinach (8 ounces)
1 tablespoon extra-virgin olive oil

1 tablespoon unsalted butter
Coarse salt

---

1 • Rinse the spinach well, drain, and put in a bowl of cold water. If using tough, curly spinach, pull off and discard the thick stems and center veins.

2 • Warm the oil and butter in a saucepan over medium-high heat until the butter melts and begins to foam. Drain the spinach quickly in a colander, leaving some water still on the leaves. Place it in the hot pan. Sprinkle with coarse salt, cover, and cook until just wilted, 2 to 3 minutes.

3 • Serve immediately.

Makes 2 servings

Easy Chocolate Mousse

To finish off the love fest, we go with the universal women's aphrodisiac . . . chocolate. Yet it's light and fluffy, nothing to weigh you down for the rest of the evening. If you know what I mean . . . wink's as good as a nod. Say no more . . . say no more. I hope you and your sweetie will love this dessert as much as we do. Funny thing, we almost never get to the dessert.

½ cup plus 2 tablespoons heavy
    cream
3 ounces good-quality semisweet or
    bittersweet chocolate, melted
    (page 42)

1 tablespoon raspberry-flavored
    liqueur or orange-flavored
    liqueur
Fresh raspberries, for serving,
    optional

1 • Using an electric mixer or whisking by hand, whip ½ cup of the cream until it holds stiff peaks.

2 • Heat the remaining 2 tablespoons cream in a small saucepan over medium heat until hot but not boiling (or heat in a microwave-safe container in the microwave oven on high power for 10 to 15 seconds).

3 • Whisk the hot cream into the melted chocolate. Add the liqueur, if using, and stir well. Using a rubber spatula, quickly fold the chocolate mixture into the whipped cream, mixing until the color is uniform throughout. You may be tempted to add more liqueur, but the flavor develops as the mousse chills.

4 • Spoon the mousse into two 8-ounce wine glasses or individual serving bowls. Cover with plastic wrap and refrigerate until the mousse is firm, at least 1 hour and up to 24 hours.

5 • Serve with fresh raspberries, if desired.

Makes 2 servings

Almond or Vanilla-Scented Chocolate Mousse

Substitute ½ teaspoon almond or vanilla extract for the liqueur and increase the amount of heavy cream that you heat and whisk into the chocolate to 3 tablespoons.

Chocolate-Dipped Strawberries

Okay, if you need a deal closer, this one is it, and it's simplicity unto itself. Red, ripe luscious strawberries combined with chocolate is a surefire winner, and it is soooooooooo easy. We went through a few fruit-chocolate combos before hitting on this one. Hint: Never try to dip a whole casaba melon. Big splatter pattern.

12 large, ripe strawberries, with leaves still attached (about ½ pound)	*3 ounces semisweet chocolate, chopped, or ½ cup semisweet chocolate chips* *1 teaspoon solid vegetable shortening, optional*

1 • Line a baking sheet with wax paper, and butter the paper.

2 • Rinse the strawberries under cold running water and pat them until they are really dry. Make sure the berries are completely dry, or the chocolate will not set up well later.

3 • Melt the chocolate (page 42). If you want the chocolate coating to be shiny, add the vegetable shortening. Stir until the chocolate is very smooth and barely warm.

4 • Hold the strawberries by their leaves and dip them, one by one, into the chocolate, leaving a narrow band at the top uncoated. Place them on the prepared baking sheet. Refrigerate for at least 30 minutes and up to 24 hours. Serve cold.

Makes 12 strawberries, or 2 servings

VARIATION

Black and White Strawberries

Dip half the berries in 1½ ounces melted semisweet chocolate and half in 1½ ounces white chocolate.

Valentine's Day Treats for Kids

If you don't want to leave out the possible results of earlier Valentine's Day celebrations, here are some great ways to get the kids involved as well.

- *Make Basic Sugar Cookies (pages 82–83), and cut them with a heart-shaped cookie cutter. Decorate unbaked cookies with small, heart-shaped, spicy cinnamon candies or candy hearts (page 84), or frost baked cookies with melted semisweet or milk chocolate (page 85).*
- *Try the Valentine's-themed Corny Crispy Rice Treats (page 257).*
- *Bake the Red Velvet Cake (pages 64–65) in two 9-inch heart-shaped pans. Frost as directed and decorate the tops of each cake with small, heart-shaped, spicy cinnamon candies, red jelly beans, or red gumdrops.*
- *Press a candy heart or a small, heart-shaped, spicy cinnamon candy into the top of each piece of Microwave Fudge (page 80) before it has completely cooled.*
- *Cover Mud Pie (pages 154–55) with whipped cream and maraschino cherries.*

Traditional St. Patrick's Day Dinner

St. Patrick's Day always meant one thing to me during my high school years. Horse poop. You see, I went to Xavier High School in downtown Manhattan. Xavier was a Jesuit, military academy. They were turning out men who would be ready for the next Crusade.

Anyway, each year, we marched in the Columbus Day Parade and the St. Patrick's Day Parade. For my first couple of years at Xavier, I was in the band. Now I'm not saying this was a judgment of the caliber of our musicianship, but we were always right behind the New York City Mounted Police Unit.

Have you ever tried to play an instrument (the flute), march, and look down at the same time? It's not easy.

So it's with those memories (and scents) in my mind that I try to conjure up a St. Patrick's Day menu. I don't think you're going to find any surprises here, nor should you. This is not a holiday that calls for nouvelle cuisine. Traditional fare, tried and true. Now, I know you're thinking, "Al, St. Patrick's Day?"

Hey, haven't you heard of the Black Irish?

Irish Stew

After a chilly morning of marching and the wearin' o' the green, what better way to warm up then a big ol' steamin' bowl of Irish Stew. And it's great to make ahead of time. In fact, it will taste better a couple of days after the snakes have returned to Ireland.

1½ cups all-purpose flour
Salt
Freshly ground pepper
3 pounds lamb stew meat, or boneless leg of lamb cut into 1½-inch cubes
⅓ cup canola oil, or other vegetable oil
3 cups canned vegetable or beef broth
1 pound pearl onions, peeled
6 medium carrots, peeled and cut into 2-inch pieces, or ¾ pound whole, peeled mini carrots

3 parsnips, peeled and cut into 2-inch pieces
2 pounds small red potatoes (2½-inch diameter), scrubbed but not peeled
1 (12-ounce) bottle dark ale
1 tablespoon thyme leaves, or 1½ teaspoons dried thyme
Chopped parsley leaves, for serving

1 • In a large resealable plastic bag, combine the flour, 1 teaspoon salt, and 1 teaspoon pepper, shaking to mix. Put half the lamb in the bag and shake to coat. Remove the meat from the bag, tapping off any excess flour. Repeat with the remaining lamb. Discard any excess flour mixture.

2 • Warm the oil in a large pot over medium-high heat. Working in batches if necessary so as not to crowd the pan, cook the lamb until well browned on all sides, 7 to 10 minutes per batch. Using a slotted spoon, remove the lamb from the pot and set it aside.

3 • Add the broth to the pot and stir, scraping up any browned bits from the bottom. Reduce the heat to medium and return the meat to the pot. Add the onions, carrots, parsnips, potatoes, and ale. Stir in the thyme and season with salt and pepper. Reduce the heat, partially cover the pot, and simmer for 1 hour, until the vegetables are tender when pierced with a knife. The stew can be cooled, covered, and refrigerated for up to

2 days or frozen, well wrapped, for up to 2 months (thaw and reheat the stew gently but thoroughly before serving).

4 • To serve, ladle the hot stew into warm, shallow bowls and sprinkle each serving with chopped parsley.

Makes 6 servings

Irish Soda Bread

This is a tasty bread that has a little bite to it thanks to the buttermilk. A perfect accompaniment to your stew.

4 cups all-purpose flour
1 tablespoon salt
¾ teaspoon baking soda

¾ teaspoon baking powder
1½ to 2 cups buttermilk

1 • Position a rack in the center of the oven and preheat the oven to 375°F. Lightly butter an 8-inch round cake pan with sides at least 1½ inches high.

2 • In a large bowl, stir together the flour, salt, baking soda, and baking powder until well mixed. Add 1½ cups of the buttermilk and stir until the mixture forms a ball. If the dough is too dry, add more buttermilk, a few spoonfuls at a time, until it comes together.

3 • Turn the dough out onto a lightly floured surface and knead for 3 minutes, until the dough is smooth and a bit elastic. Form it into a slightly flattened round loaf about 7 inches in diameter and place it in the prepared pan. Using a sharp knife, make a shallow X on the top.

4 • Bake the bread for 40 to 45 minutes, until golden and hollow-sounding when tapped. Remove the pan from the oven and transfer the loaf to a wire rack to cool at least slightly.

5 • The bread is best served warm or at room temperature shortly after it is made; cut into 8 wedges or slice. If making ahead, let cool completely, and then use a serrated knife to cut the bread crosswise into ¾-inch slices, wrap each slice well, and freeze for up to 1 month; to serve the bread, unwrap and toast it, frozen, in a toaster or under the broiler until it is golden brown and hot.

Makes one 7-inch round loaf

Bread Pudding
with Whiskey Sauce

Okay, it's St. Patrick's Day. You are not getting off easy with this meal. If you thought we might lighten things up with dessert, you're full of the Blarney. And in keeping with the day, we're going with a whiskey sauce. Just don't forget to make the bread pudding!

FOR THE PUDDING

2 tablespoons unsalted butter, softened (page 25)
1 (12-ounce) loaf day-old French or Italian bread, torn into bite-size chunks
1 quart half-and-half, light cream, or whole milk

3 large eggs
2¼ cups sugar
½ cup golden raisins, dried cranberries, or dried cherries
1 tablespoon pure vanilla extract
2 tablespoons finely grated orange zest (from 2 to 3 oranges)

1 • Position a rack in the center of the oven and preheat the oven to 350°F. With a pastry brush, spread the softened butter evenly over the bottom and sides of a 9 by 13-inch baking dish with sides at least 1½ inches high. Set aside.

2 • Put the chunks of bread into a large bowl and add the half-and-half. When the bread is soft, crumble it with your fingers and continue soaking until all of the liquid is absorbed (the bread will be very soggy).

3 • In a separate bowl, using a wire whisk, beat the eggs and sugar until smooth and thick, about 3 minutes. Stir in the raisins, vanilla, and orange zest. Pour the egg mixture over the bread mixture and stir until well combined.

4 • Pour the mixture into the prepared dish, spreading evenly with a rubber spatula. The pudding can be covered and refrigerated for up to 24 hours (Bring to room temperature before proceeding).

5 • Place the baking dish in larger roasting pan and transfer to the oven. Carefully pour

boiling water into the roasting pan to a depth of about 1 inch. Bake the pudding for about 1 hour, or until a knife inserted in the center comes out clean. While the pudding is baking, prepare the sauce.

FOR THE WHISKEY SAUCE

8 tablespoons (1 stick) unsalted
    butter, cut into ½-inch pieces
1 cup sugar

1 large egg
Pinch of salt
½ cup Irish whiskey or bourbon

1 • Melt the butter in a double boiler. In a bowl, beat the sugar, egg, and salt together with a whisk. Add this mixture to the melted butter, and cook, stirring constantly with a wooden spoon until the sugar dissolves completely and the mixture coats the back of the spoon, about 5 minutes. Remove from the heat and stir in the whiskey. The sauce will by quite runny. The sauce can be cooled and refrigerated in a heatproof jar for up to 2 days.

2 • If the sauce was refrigerated, reheat the jar of sauce in a saucepan of simmering water, stirring occasionally, until the sauce is heated through, or microwave (make sure to remove any metal lids) at half power for about 2 minutes, stirring halfway through.

3 • Serve the pudding warm or at room temperature, spooning it into shallow bowls and topping each serving with a spoonful of warm whiskey sauce.

Makes 8 servings

Easter Celebration

For the girls in our house, Easter was always a favorite holiday. They got new dresses and shoes. Of course, new shoes and clothes meant shopping. To a preteen boy, there is nothing worse than going shopping with your mother and sisters.

Not only was it boring, but I had to keep an eye peeled to make sure none of my friends saw me. Odds were, if they were there in Montgomery Ward or Gimbels, their sisters and mothers had them in the death grip of retail hell as well.

Once the shopping had been completed and we were all outfitted with new Sunday best, the next stop was the grocery store. My mom would have a long list of food to buy for our Easter Sunday feast, which usually included a leg of lamb, a chicken, and various sides.

If you're a kid, food is not the centerpiece of Easter. Candy is. Easter means little chocolate Easter eggs, marshmallow Peeps, malted milk chocolate eggs, and of course the focal point: The Big Daddy chocolate Easter Bunny. It was always a fight to see who would bite the head off first. I, being the oldest, saw it as my birthright. And yet, my younger siblings saw it as their sworn duty to beat me to it.

So, remember, if you've got kids, don't worry about them eating. They're probably lolling around the ceiling somewhere, hopped up on cocoa and sugar. And they're not comin' down for a couple of days.

Spring Salad

Everyone says they're eating more healthfully these days, so I include a couple of salads here. And folks will, indeed, take a spoonful or two to be polite and give credence to the lie. If I were you, I wouldn't double this recipe, unless, of course, you're hosting a vegetarian Easter.

FOR THE DRESSING

½ cup chopped chives
3 tablespoons lemon juice (from
   1 lemon)
3 cloves garlic, peeled and coarsely
   chopped

¼ teaspoon sugar
¼ teaspoon salt
¼ teaspoon freshly ground pepper
¾ cup extra-virgin olive oil

In a blender, puree the chives, lemon juice, garlic, sugar, salt, and pepper. With the machine on, slowly pour in the oil, so that it is incorporated into the dressing and makes an emulsion. Let sit for at least 30 minutes for the flavors to blend, or cover and refrigerate for up to 2 days.

FOR THE SALAD

12 cups mixed greens, such as spinach, arugula, watercress, and lettuces (about 6 ounces)
8 medium radishes, thinly sliced
8 scallions, white and green parts, chopped

Place the greens, radishes, and scallions in a serving bowl. Drizzle some of the dressing on top and toss to coat lightly.

Makes 8 servings

Asparagus Salad
with Lemon and Tarragon

Okay, I have asked everybody remotely related to cooking and the food industry. No one can tell me why eating asparagus is readily apparent when you go to the bathroom just ten minutes after eating the stuff. What the heck is in asparagus?

½ cup plain yogurt
3 tablespoons mayonnaise
1 shallot, peeled and finely chopped
2 tablespoons lemon juice (from 1
    lemon)

2 teaspoons chopped tarragon leaves,
    or 1 teaspoon dried tarragon
Salt
Freshly ground pepper
2 pounds asparagus, trimmed

1 • In a small bowl, combine the yogurt, mayonnaise, shallot, lemon juice, and tarragon and season with salt and pepper. Stir to mix well. Cover and refrigerate for at least 1 hour and up to 2 days.

2 • Several hours before you are going to serve the asparagus, put them in a large skillet with enough cold water to cover them. Salt the water. Bring to a boil over medium-high heat, and then reduce the heat and simmer until the thickest part of the stalks can be pierced with a fork, 4 to 8 minutes, depending on the thickness of the asparagus. Using a slotted spoon, transfer the asparagus to a colander and run them under cold water to stop the cooking. Drain and transfer to a serving platter. The asparagus can be covered and refrigerated for up to 8 hours.

3 • About 30 minutes before you plan to serve the salad, pour the dressing over the asparagus. Serve at room temperature.

Makes 8 servings

Roast Leg of Lamb with Garlic and Herbs

I like a leg of lamb with the bone-in. I think the flavor's better and it cooks quicker. And there are few better smells than leg of lamb roasting in the oven with some garlic slivers stuck inside.

One (6- to 8-pound) bone-in leg
   of lamb
2 cloves garlic, peeled and cut into
   slivers
½ cup extra-virgin olive oil
½ cup lemon juice (from 2 to 3 lemons)
4 teaspoons chopped oregano leaves,
   or 2 teaspoons dried oregano

4 teaspoons thyme leaves, or
   2 teaspoons dried thyme
1 tablespoon chopped rosemary
   leaves, or 2 teaspoons dried
   rosemary
Salt
Freshly ground pepper

1 • Rinse the lamb under cold running water and pat it dry with paper towels. Using a small, sharp knife, cut a dozen small slits in the meat. Tuck the garlic slivers into the slits. Place the meat in a shallow dish.

2 • In a small bowl, stir together the oil, lemon juice, oregano, thyme, rosemary, 1 teaspoon salt, and 1 teaspoon pepper. Pour the marinade over the lamb and turn to coat. Cover with plastic wrap and refrigerate for at least 8 hours and up to 24 hours, basting with the marinade as often as is practical.

3 • Remove the lamb from the refrigerator, uncover it, and let sit at room temperature for at least 30 minutes. Position a rack in the oven so that the lamb in a roasting pan will fit. Preheat the oven to 325°F. Lightly oil a roasting pan fitted with a rack (oiling the pan will help keep the pan drippings from sticking).

4 • Transfer the lamb to the rack in the prepared pan, reserving the leftover marinade. Season the meat with salt and pepper. Roast the lamb, basting every 20 to 30 minutes, first with the reserved marinade, and then with the juices that accumulate in the pan. The lamb will need to cook for about 20 minutes per pound, or between 2 hours for a

6-pound leg of lamb and 2 hours and 40 minutes for an 8-pound leg of lamb. The lamb is done when a meat thermometer or an instant-read thermometer inserted in the thickest part of the meat (not touching the bone) registers at least 145°F for medium-rare.

5 • Remove the pan from the oven and transfer the lamb to a cutting board. Cover it with a piece of aluminum foil to keep warm and let rest for 20 minutes before carving. Pour the pan juices into a glass measure or gravy skimmer; spoon off any fat that rises to the top and discard. Cover the juices and keep warm while the lamb rests. Add any juices that collect as the lamb sits.

6 • Carve the lamb and arrange the slices on a large warm platter, drizzling them with the pan juices just before serving.

Makes 8 to 10 servings

Glazed Baked Ham

You can't go wrong with a ham. I usually buy one of those spiral sliced hams, like a honey-baked ham, and then add my own glaze on top of what they already have. I like the ready-cooked ones because they save time. And left-over ham goes great with those hard-boiled eggs that your kids didn't find.

1 (5- to 7-pound) partially or fully cooked ham	Glaze of your choice (see opposite)

1 • Position a rack in the oven so that the ham in a roasting pan will fit. Preheat the oven to 325°F. Lightly oil a shallow roasting pan (oiling the pan will help keep the ham from sticking). Place the ham cut side down in the prepared pan.

2 • *If you bought a fully cooked ham,* bake it for 10 to 12 minutes per pound, or between 50 and 60 minutes for a 5-pound ham, and between 1 hour and 10 minutes and 1 hour and 25 minutes for a 7-pound ham. The ham is done when a meat thermometer or an instant-read thermometer inserted in the thickest part of the meat (not touching a bone) registers at least 140°F. *If you bought a partially cooked ham,* bake it for 15 to 20 minutes a pound, or between 1 hour and 15 minutes and 1 hour and 40 minutes for a 5-pound ham, and between 1 hour and 45 minutes and 2 hours and 20 minutes for a 7-pound ham. The ham is done when a meat thermometer or an instant-read thermometer inserted in the thickest part of the meat registers at least 160°F.

3 • Remove the ham from the oven about 45 minutes before you estimate that it will be done, and spoon or brush the glaze over the top and sides. Return to the oven and bake until done, basting occasionally with any remaining glaze or the pan juices. Remove the ham from oven, cover loosely with aluminum foil to keep warm, and let rest for 10 to 15 minutes before carving.

4 • Slice the ham and arrange it on a warm serving platter and drizzle any pan juices on top.

Makes 10 to 14 servings

RUM GLAZE

¼ cup dark brown sugar
¼ cup dark rum
¼ cup red wine, cooking sherry,
    Madeira, or red (sweet) vermouth

¼ cup orange marmalade
¼ teaspoon ground cloves

In a small bowl, whisk together all of the ingredients. Use immediately or cover and refrigerate for up to 5 days.

Makes about 1 cup, or enough for at least 7 pounds of ham

CHUTNEY-MUSTARD GLAZE

½ cup mango chutney
¼ cup Dijon mustard

¼ cup pineapple juice

In a small bowl, whisk together all of the ingredients. Use immediately or cover and refrigerate for up to 5 days.

Makes about 1 cup, or enough for at least 7 pounds of ham

GINGER-CURRANT GLAZE

1 cup red currant jelly

1 tablespoon peeled, chopped fresh ginger

In a small saucepan, warm the jelly with the ginger until the jelly has liquefied. Use immediately.

Makes about 1 cup, or enough for at least 7 pounds of ham

Easter Leftovers

Gotta love the leftovers, especially at Easter time. Forget about turkey, lamb and ham make for tasty reruns.

LAMB IN PITA POCKETS

Make a thick sauce of 1 cup plain yogurt; ½ cucumber, peeled, seeded, and grated; 2 teaspoons lemon juice; and chopped fresh mint. Season with salt and pepper. Toss 18 thin slices cooked lamb with the sauce. Cut three 8-inch pita bread pockets in half crosswise, and separate the sides of the bread to make pockets. Stuff the pita pockets with the lamb, sliced red onions, sliced tomatoes, and several leaves of spinach, arugula, or watercress. Makes 6 servings.

LAMB AND BARLEY SOUP

Put the lamb bone and 2 quarts of water in a large pot. Bring to a boil, then reduce the heat and simmer for 2 hours. Remove the bone, slice off any meat and return the meat to the pot with ¾ cup barley, 4 sliced carrots, 2 sliced medium onions, and 3 tablespoons tomato paste. Season with salt and pepper and simmer until the barley is plump and tender, 30 to 40 minutes. Serve hot. Makes 8 servings.

HAM-STUFFED PEPPERS

Cut 4 bell peppers in half lengthwise and remove the seeds. Place them cut side up in a baking dish and pour boiling water on top to cover; let sit for 5 to 10 minutes. Meanwhile, cook 1 medium onion in 2 tablespoons of olive oil in a large skillet over medium-high heat. Add 2½ cups finely chopped ham, ¼ cup chopped parsley leaves, ⅓ cup bread crumbs (page 141), 1 egg, and a few tablespoons of tomato juice to moisten. Drain the pepper halves and fill them with the stuffing. Place them in a baking dish and pour in tomato juice to a depth of ¼ inch to keep the peppers moist. Dot the stuffed peppers with butter and bake, uncovered, in a preheated 350°F oven for 25 to 30 minutes, until the tops are beginning to brown. Makes 8 servings.

HOT SPLIT PEA SOUP (PAGE 147)

Use a ham bone to flavor the soup; the more meat on it the better.

Pan-Glazed Carrots

My little girl, Leila, loves these carrots. She thinks they're dessert. Who am I to dissuade her?

2 pounds whole, peeled mini carrots	*4 teaspoons chopped dill leaves, or*
3 tablespoons unsalted butter	*2 teaspoons dried dill*
3 tablespoons honey	*Salt*
	Freshly ground pepper

1 • Place the carrots in a large skillet and cover them with cold water. Salt the water. Bring to a boil over high heat, reduce the heat, and simmer until the carrots can just be pierced with a knife, about 4 minutes. Drain well. The carrots can be cooled, covered, and refrigerated for up to 24 hours.

2 • Dry the skillet, add the butter, and melt over medium-high heat. When it begins to foam, add the honey and stir. Add the carrots and cook, turning, until they are coated. Sprinkle with the dill, season with salt and pepper, and cook for a few minutes more, until the carrots are very tender.

3 • Spoon into a warm bowl and serve.

Makes 8 servings

Roasted Baby Potatoes

I cannot think of a better side for a great leg of lamb than these potatoes. They are simple yet satisfying. Much like myself.

---

4 tablespoons extra-virgin olive oil
2 pounds small red potatoes (2½-inch diameter), scrubbed but not peeled

Coarse salt
Freshly ground pepper

---

1 • Position a rack in the center of the oven and preheat the oven to 325°F. Use 1 tablespoon of the oil to lightly coat two 9 by 13-inch baking dishes with sides at least 1½ inches high.

2 • Divide the potatoes between the prepared dishes and drizzle them with the remaining 3 tablespoons oil. Season generously with salt and pepper. Toss to coat.

3 • Roast the potatoes for about 1½ hours, turning once, until they can be easily pierced with a knife and are nicely browned. Serve hot.

Makes 8 servings

NOTE: This recipe is designed to complement the roast lamb or ham, which are well seasoned, and to cook along with the ham or lamb at 325°F (you should be able to fit the baking dishes under the rack where the meat is cooking). If serving with other main courses, you may choose to season the potatoes with chopped garlic and/or chopped herbs (rosemary and thyme work well). You can also increase the oven temperature to 425°F and decrease roasting time to 50 to 60 minutes.

Peas and Mint

Talk about a little spring surprise. I think that when your guests first bite into these peas, the smile on their face will linger awhile. No one expects the flavors this dish brings to the table.

5 tablespoons unsalted butter	Salt
¼ cup mint jelly	Freshly ground pepper
1½ pounds frozen peas, preferably	1 tablespoon chopped mint leaves,
"petits pois" or tiny peas	optional

1 • Melt the butter in a large saucepan over medium-high heat until it begins to foam. Add the mint jelly and stir until it liquefies. Add the peas, season with salt and pepper, cover, and cook, stirring once or twice, until tender but still bright green, 3 to 5 minutes.

2 • Transfer the peas to a warm serving bowl and garnish with chopped mint if desired. Serve hot.

Makes 8 servings

Lemon Pie

A great pie that can be made relatively quickly if you use a store-bought crust, this has sweet and tart all in one bite. And it can be served warm or chilled. Come to think of it, this pie is a lot like my ex-wife. Just kidding.

FOR THE CRUST

1 unbaked, store-bought, single (9-inch) pie crust

or

1 cup sliced almonds
¾ cup all-purpose flour
⅓ cup sugar
¼ teaspoon salt
½ teaspoon almond extract
6 tablespoons (¾ stick) unsalted butter, softened (page 25)
1 to 2 tablespoons ice water, if needed

1 • If using a store-bought crust, preheat the oven to 425°F. Fit the pastry into a 9-inch pie plate, cover with foil, and place dried beans, rice, or pie weights on top of the foil to keep the crust from puffing up. Partially bake the pie shell for 10 to 12 minutes, until firm but still pale. Remove the pie weights and the foil, and let cool slightly before filling.

2 • If making the crust, position a rack in the center of the oven and preheat the oven to 400°F. Generously butter a 9-inch pie plate.

3 • Using a food processor or clean coffee grinder, chop the almonds finely, making sure to stop before they become "almond butter." *If using a food processor,* pulse the chopped nuts, flour, sugar, and salt to blend. Add the almond extract and pulse, then add the butter, 1 tablespoon at a time, and pulse just until a dough forms. If needed, add the water, 1 teaspoon at a time, pulsing until the dough comes together. *If mixing by hand,* stir together the nuts, flour, sugar, and salt in a large bowl. Stir in the almond extract, and then cut in the butter with a pastry blender or 2 knives, mixing until a dough forms. If needed, add the water, 1 teaspoon at a time, mixing until the dough comes together. The dough can be wrapped in plastic wrap and refrigerated for up to 2 days or frozen for up to 1 month; before using, let sit at room temperature until pliable.

4 • Press the dough into the prepared pie plate. Cover the crust loosely with aluminum foil (if you cover it tightly, the foil will stick to the crust) and bake for 8 minutes. Remove the foil and bake for another 5 minutes, until the crust is beginning to turn golden in color. Remove the crust from the oven and let cool slightly.

FOR THE FILLING

8 tablespoons (1 stick) unsalted
    butter, cut into chunks
3 large eggs
3 large egg yolks
1 cup sugar

Pinch of salt
½ cup lemon juice (from 2 to
    3 lemons)
½ teaspoon pure vanilla extract

Combine the butter, eggs, egg yolks, sugar, and salt in a double boiler and cook, whisking until quite thick, for about 5 minutes. Remove from the heat and stir in the lemon juice and vanilla.

TO BAKE

1 large egg yolk, lightly beaten

1 • Reduce the oven temperature to 325°F.
2 • Using a pastry brush, lightly coat the partially baked crust with the beaten egg yolk. Scrape the filling into the crust. Bend thin strips of aluminum foil over the exposed crust on the edge of the pie plate to prevent overbrowning.
3 • Bake the pie for 15 to 20 minutes, until the filling is set. It will still be jiggly, like gelatin, but the top will have colored slightly and a knife inserted in the center will come out clean. Remove the pie from the oven, discard the foil strips, and place the pie on a wire rack to cool at least partially. Once cool, the pie can be covered with plastic wrap and refrigerated for up to 1 day.

TO SERVE

2 tablespoons confectioners' sugar

1 • Serve the pie warm, at room temperature, or chilled. Just before serving, sift the confectioners' sugar over the top, then slice the pie into 8 wedges.

Makes one 9-inch pie, or 8 servings

Meringue Berry Basket

This is the dessert version of soup in a bread bowl. Remember that *Seinfeld* episode when George's boss, Yankees' owner George Steinbrenner was going on about soup in a bowl made out of bread? First you eat the soup, then you eat the bread, next thing you know, you're looking at your desk.

Same idea with this meringue berry basket. It's an edible basket that can be eaten with the berries. In fact, I was thinking about a recipe for meringue spoons, but decided that might be too much.

FOR THE MERINGUE

Nonstick cooking spray
4 large egg whites
½ teaspoon cream of tartar

1 cup sugar
1 teaspoon pure vanilla extract

1 • Position a rack in the center of the oven and preheat the oven to 250°F. Use a cake pan or a plate to draw a 9-inch circle on a piece of parchment paper. Turn the paper over and place it on a baking sheet—you should be able to see the circle through the paper. Very lightly spray the paper with nonstick cooking spray.

2 • In a large, very clean bowl (any trace of grease will keep the whites from whipping to their fullest volume), whip the egg whites with an electric mixer at high speed until frothy. Add the cream of tartar and beat in. Gradually add ¼ cup of the sugar, beating constantly. Continue beating until the egg whites are glossy and hold medium peaks.

3 • Sprinkle the remaining ¾ cup sugar over the top of the whites. Using a rubber spatula, fold the sugar in gently, using a sweeping motion to lift and stir the meringue. Add the vanilla and continue folding the mixture until it holds stiff peaks, about 1 minute.

4 • Spoon the meringue into the center of the circle. Use the spatula to spread out the meringue to the circle's edge. Drag the spatula from the center to the side to create a well in the center and build up the sides 1 to 1½ inches high, creating a shallow bowl shape.

5 • Bake the meringue until firm and pale beige in color, about 1 hour. Remove the pan from

the oven and place on a wire rack to cool. When cool, carefully peel the parchment off the bottom of the meringue (it is fragile). The meringue can be stored in an airtight container at room temperature for up to 1 day. (If you don't have a large enough container, store the meringue in the oven once the oven has cooled.) Gently transfer the meringue to a serving plate.

FOR THE FILLING

4 cups fresh or frozen strawberries	*1 cup heavy cream*
Sugar, if needed	*1 teaspoon pure vanilla extract*

1 • If using fresh berries, rinse, hull, and slice them. If using frozen berries, thaw them according to package directions. Sprinkle the strawberries with a little sugar if you think they aren't quite sweet enough, keeping in mind that the meringue is rather sweet.
2 • Using an electric mixer or whisking by hand, whip the heavy cream until it holds soft peaks. Add the vanilla and 2 teaspoons sugar, if desired, and whip until the cream holds stiff peaks.
3 • Spoon the strawberries into the meringue just before serving (if the berries sit in the meringue for too long, the meringue will get soggy). Using a serrated knife, slice the meringue into 8 wedges and carefully transfer them to individual dessert plates. Top each serving with a dollop of whipped cream.

Makes 8 servings

VARIATION

Tropical Meringue Basket

Substitute ¼ teaspoon ground cinnamon and ½ teaspoon ground ginger for the vanilla extract in the meringue. Substitute 2 diced, peeled mangoes for half of the strawberries and season the fruit with a bit of grated lemon zest and sugar.

Mother's Day Breakfast
in Bed

Okay, moms, hand the book over to the father of your children right now. This is a Dad-kids kinda thing. There are few things more fun than cooking with your children.

Courtney still has a love of cooking, one that began when she was much smaller. Not only did she excel at the stove, she was very much into the presentation. She would go pick flowers from the yard to decorate the plates and place settings.

Leila is following in her sister's footsteps. A budding chef in her own right, she loves to help mix the pancake, cookie, and cake batter. Truth be told, she loves to taste the pancake, cookie, and cake batter. But it's a start. And there is such pride in your children's eyes when they know that they helped make breakfast for Mommy.

Then, afterwards, don't forget . . . Daddy and the kids shouldn't leave the kitchen cleanup to Mommy. Not if daddy wants to reap the rewards of planning such a nice breakfast.

Sparkling Cocktail

Since the kids are present, this is a great alternative to a real mimosa. But the fizziness will still say "sophistication" to your little gourmands.

1 quart orange juice, chilled
2½ cups sparkling white grape juice, chilled

2 tablespoons lemon juice (from 1 lemon)
Ice cubes, for serving
1 orange, halved and sliced, for serving

Just before serving, mix together the orange, grape, and lemon juices in a 2-quart pitcher. Serve over ice, garnished with a slice or two of orange.

Makes about 1½ quarts, or six 8-ounce servings

Overnight French Toast

So that you're not running around like crazy prepping breakfast Mother's Day morning, here's a dish you can make the night before. Daddy needs to have a plan if he's gonna survive.

About 12 (½-inch-thick) slices white bread
½ cup raspberry or strawberry jam
4 large eggs
1¾ cups whole milk
2 tablespoons sugar

2 teaspoons pure vanilla extract
1 teaspoon ground cinnamon
¼ teaspoon baking powder
⅛ teaspoon salt
Confectioners' sugar or pure maple syrup, for serving

1 • Lightly butter an 8-inch square baking dish with sides at least 1½ inches high. Place about 4 slices of bread in a single layer in the bottom of the prepared dish. You may have to cut some of the pieces in half to create a snug fit.

2 • Spread ¼ cup of the jam over the layer of bread. Place another layer of bread over the jam and spread this second layer with the remaining ¼ cup jam. Fit a third layer of bread on top.

3 • In a large bowl, whisk together the eggs, milk, sugar, vanilla, cinnamon, baking powder, and salt until well blended. Pour the mixture slowly over the bread, allowing the bread to absorb some of the liquid as you pour. Cover the entire baking dish with plastic wrap and refrigerate for at least 8 hours and up to 12 hours.

4 • Position a rack in the center of the oven and preheat the oven to 375°F.

5 • Bake the French toast, uncovered, until the egg mixture is set and the bread is puffed and golden, about 50 minutes. Transfer the baking dish to a wire rack and let cool for 5 to 10 minutes.

6 • Cut the French toast into 6 squares, each 2½ by 4 inches, and carefully transfer to individual plates. Sprinkle with confectioners' sugar, or serve with warm maple syrup.

Makes 6 servings

Baked Eggs with Salsa

Salsa has surpassed ketchup as the number one condiment in America. Latin flava is hot right now, so why not on Mother's Day? Hey, if it's worked for J-Lo, it can work for you.

FOR THE SALSA

1 (16-ounce jar) chunky store-bought salsa (1½ cups), mild, medium or hot, according to your taste

or

2 medium tomatoes (about ¾ pound), stemmed, cored, seeded, and finely chopped

¼ green bell pepper, stemmed, seeded, and finely chopped

1 fresh or canned jalapeño pepper, stemmed, seeded, and finely chopped

1 clove garlic, peeled and minced

2 tablespoons chopped cilantro leaves, optional

1 teaspoon lime or lemon juice

1 teaspoon extra-virgin olive oil

1 teaspoon cider vinegar

½ teaspoon salt

½ teaspoons freshly ground pepper

Combine all of the ingredients in a small bowl. Cover and let sit for at least 30 minutes for the flavors to blend, or cover and refrigerate for up to 2 days.

FOR THE EGGS

6 large eggs

3 ounces grated Monterey Jack or cheddar cheese (¾ cup)

1 • Position a rack in the center of the oven and preheat the oven to 400°F.

2 • Lightly oil six 6-ounce ramekins and place them on a baking sheet.

3 • Spoon ¼ cup salsa into each ramekin. Crack an egg on top of the salsa in each ramekin. Sprinkle 2 tablespoons of cheese over each egg.

4 • Bake for 15 to 20 minutes, until the eggs are firm and the cheese is puffed and beginning to brown; the yolks will be set but not hard.

5 • Place each ramekin on a plate and serve immediately.

Makes 6 servings

Home Fries

Mmmmmm. Home fries. Chances are your wife is not thinking about eating home fries. She's thinking she wants you to keep the kids a little while longer so she can go work out. However, you and the kids'll be eating, too. And home fries smell soooooo good when they're cooking.

3 pounds Yukon gold or other yellow potatoes (about 8 medium), peeled and cut into 1-inch chunks
3 tablespoons unsalted butter
3 tablespoons extra-virgin olive oil

1 medium onion, peeled and sliced
½ medium red onion, peeled and sliced
Salt
Freshly ground pepper

1 • Pour 2 to 3 inches of water into a large pot and bring to a boil over high heat. Set the potatoes in a steamer basket over the boiling water, taking care that the potatoes are not sitting in the water. Cover and steam the potatoes until they can be just pierced with a knife, about 12 minutes (do not overcook; they will cook more, later on, in the skillet). Remove the potatoes from the pot and set aside. The potatoes can be cooled, covered, and refrigerated for up to 24 hours.

2 • Melt the butter in the oil in a large, preferably nonstick, skillet over medium heat until the butter begins to foam. Add the onion and cook, stirring, until softened and beginning to color, about 7 minutes. Using a slotted spoon, remove the onions from the pan and set them aside. Add the potatoes to the skillet, season with salt and pepper, and brown on one side for about 20 minutes, stirring as little as possible and reducing the heat, if necessary, to keep them from burning. Turn the potatoes, return the onions to the pan, and cook for about 15 minutes more, until the potatoes are well browned and beginning to crisp. Season again with salt and pepper.

3 • Serve the potatoes immediately, or let sit, uncovered, at room temperature for several hours and reheat in the skillet over low heat. Serve hot.

Makes 6 servings

Breakfast Meats

I have always looked at Sunday as the BIG BREAKFAST morning. My dad was a believer in that concept. He took over breakfast on Sundays. Grits, eggs, bacon, pancakes, sausage, and toast. I like to continue that tradition . . . so let's talk meat.

Bacon: Plan on 3 slices per serving. The safest way for kids to cook bacon is in the microwave oven, where it won't splatter hot bacon fat everywhere. Separate the slices and place them on several layers of paper towels on a microwave-safe plate. Cover with more towels. Microwave on high power for 2 minutes, then check; if the bacon is crisp, it is done. If not, continue to microwave, checking at 1-minute intervals. (The time will vary according to the power of your microwave and the thickness of the bacon, but won't take more than 5 minutes total.) You can also cook the bacon by starting it in a cold skillet over medium heat for about 15 minutes, or broil 5 inches from the heat source, turning often, for 10 to 15 minutes. A toaster oven works well for small quantities.

Breakfast sausage: If cooking frozen links, follow the package directions. For loose sausage, form it into 3-inch patties about ¾ inch thick, calculating 2 patties per person. Brown the sausage in a lightly greased skillet over medium-high heat for about 15 minutes, turning halfway through, until the sausage is crisp on the outside. Transfer 1 patty from the pan to a cutting board and slice; it should be brown throughout. If still pink, return it to the skillet and cook, checking at 2- or 3-minute intervals.

Ham or Canadian bacon: Figure 2 slices per serving. Cook in a lightly oiled skillet over medium-high heat until the slices begin to color, about 5 minutes per side.

Broiled Honey-Ginger Grapefruit

Here's how you can take an ordinary breakfast fruit and turn it into something special. Isn't that special?

3 pink grapefruits	¾ teaspoon ground ginger
3 tablespoons honey	

1 • Position a rack so that it is 4 to 5 inches from the heat source of your broiler. Preheat the broiler.

2 • Cut each grapefruit in half crosswise and cut a very thin slice off the bottom of each half so that it will sit level on a flat surface. Using a grapefruit knife or sharp paring knife, loosen the pulp from the peel by running the knife around the inside edge. Run the knife down each of the membranes dividing the grapefruit sections. Place the grapefruit halves cut side up in a 9 by 13-inch baking dish with sides at least 1½ inches high.

3 • In a small bowl, stir together the honey and ginger. Using a spoon, drizzle some of the mixture over the top of each grapefruit half.

4 • Broil until the grapefruit is hot throughout and the top begins to color, 3 to 5 minutes.

5 • Serve immediately.

Makes 6 servings

Man-Pleasin' Father's Day Meal

Did you know that several telephone companies say Mother's Day is the busiest day for long-distance calls? The flip side is that more collect calls are made on Father's Day than on any other day of the year. Nice, huh?

But Dads are making a comeback. In 1993, a consumer-spending poll showed that for the first time, people said they were going to spend more on Father's Day gifts than they were on Mother's Day trinkets. I guess that just means the price of ugly ties went up higher than the cost of really fragrant candles.

As a kid, I knew that the best thing I could give my Dad was something I made. He got more than his fair share of misshapen ashtrays and cufflink holders. Yet each one was met with a heartfelt expression of thanks. It's funny, we never thought about making our father breakfast in bed, only Mom. We never really thought about cooking for Dad.

Well that's about to change. Kids love to cook. They love to make things for their parents. What better day to combine the two loves?

So, guys, if you're reading this chapter, pass the book over to your wife. It's your day. Which means you most likely spent the morning playing golf, basketball, or washing the car. So the heck with breakfast. It's lunch or dinnertime. It's your day. You are king of the castle. Allow your family to serve you . . . Oh, there's the phone. Hey, it's collect. You can thank 'em for the tie!

Deviled Eggs

Manly foods hold sway today. Big eats. Food that requires very little in the way of utensils, cutlery, or plates. So let's get it on.

12 large eggs	Freshly ground pepper
½ cup mayonnaise	Chopped chives, parsley, or tarragon
1 tablespoon Dijon mustard	leaves, for serving, optional
Salt	

1 • Put the eggs in a saucepan large enough to hold them in 1 layer, and add enough cold water to cover them by 1 inch. Bring the water almost to a boil over medium-high heat. When you see bubbles forming at the edge of the pan, shut the heat off, cover the pot, and let the eggs sit in the hot water for 15 minutes. Remove the eggs carefully from the pan and let cool, but do not let them sit at room temperature for more than 2 hours. The eggs can be refrigerated for up to 4 days.

2 • Gently crack the shells and peel each egg. Cut each egg in half lengthwise. Scrape the yolks into a bowl and keep the cooked whites intact.

3 • Add the mayonnaise and mustard to the egg yolks and season with salt and pepper. Stir with a fork to mix well.

4 • Using a teaspoon, fill each egg white half with the yolk mixture. Garnish with chives, parsley, or tarragon, if desired. Serve immediately or cover and refrigerate for several hours and serve chilled.

Makes 8 servings

VARIATION

Curried Deviled Eggs

Omit the mustard and add 2 tablespoons curry powder and 2 teaspoons lemon juice to the yolk mixture.

Seven-Layer Dip

Okay, between the deviled eggs and this dip, you'll be hearing from this menu for a while. Make sure you've got good cross ventilation in your bedroom. Then bring on the seven-layer dip. Only eating utensil needed . . . big ol' tortilla chips.

1 (16-ounce) can refried beans
3 large ripe avocados, peeled and
    pitted
2 tablespoons lime or lemon juice
    (from 1 to 2 limes or 1 lemon)
2 cups sour cream
1 (1-ounce) envelope taco seasoning
1 (7-ounce) can mild green chile
    peppers, drained and chopped

1 (3.8-ounce) can sliced black olives,
    drained
4 medium tomatoes (1 pound),
    stemmed, cored, seeded, and
    diced
8 ounces grated Monterey Jack
    cheese (2 cups)
1/4 cup chopped cilantro leaves
Tortilla chips, for serving

1 • Spoon the beans into the bottom of a lightly oiled 9 by 13-inch baking dish with sides at least 1½ inches high. Smooth the beans into an even layer using a table knife or a flat metal spatula.

2 • In a small bowl, using a potato masher or fork, mash the avocados with the lime juice. Spoon this mixture over the beans.

3 • In another bowl, mix the sour cream and taco seasoning, stirring well to distribute the seasoning. Spoon over the avocado layer.

4 • Sprinkle the chiles over the sour cream, sprinkle the olives over the chiles, top with the tomatoes, and finish with a layer of the cheese. The dish can be covered and refrigerated for up to 24 hours (return to room temperature before broiling).

5 • Position a rack so that it is about 4 inches from the heat source of your broiler. Preheat the broiler.

6 • Broil the dip just until the cheese melts and begins to brown in spots, 4 to 6 minutes. Sprinkle with the chopped cilantro and serve hot, with tortilla chips for dipping.

Makes at least 10 servings

Mixed Grill

I like this recipe. It's a big buffet of meat. There isn't a meat that a man isn't gonna like in this dish. Vegetarians, avert your eyes.

2 T-bone steaks (1 pound each)
1½ pounds center-cut loin pork chops
    (3 chops)
1½ pounds center-cut loin lamb chops
    (3 chops)
1 pound Italian sausage, hot or mild,
    separated into individual links
    (6 links)
1 cup extra-virgin olive oil

⅓ cup lemon juice (from 2 lemons)
4 cloves garlic, peeled and finely
    chopped
2 tablespoons mixed chopped herbs,
    such as basil, rosemary, and
    oregano
¾ teaspoon salt
½ teaspoon freshly ground pepper

1 • Rinse the steaks, pork, and lamb under cold running water and pat them dry with paper towels. Combine with the sausage in a shallow pan.

2 • In a bowl or jar, combine the olive oil, lemon juice, garlic, herbs, salt, and pepper. Stir or shake to mix well.

3 • Pour ¾ to 1 cup of the marinade over the meat, turning the meat to coat. Cover and refrigerate for at least 8 hours and up to 24 hours, turning the meat once during this time. Cover and refrigerate the remaining marinade to serve as a sauce with the meat. Remove the meat from the refrigerator and let sit at room temperature for about 30 minutes before grilling.

4 • Prepare a charcoal fire or preheat a gas grill for direct grilling over high heat (400°F to 500°F).

5 • Remove the meat from the marinade and discard the marinade. Pierce each sausage link several times with a fork. Grill the meat for 12 to 15 minutes, turning once. An instant-read thermometer inserted in the center of the steak and lamb should register at least 145°F for medium-rare; the pork and sausage should register at least 160°F. Transfer the meat to a cutting board, cover with aluminum foil to keep warm, and let rest for 5 minutes. Slice the steak, pork, and lamb off the bones, and slice the sausage links in half.

6 • Arrange the meat on a warm platter and serve immediately. Use the reserved herb marinade as a sauce along with any or all of the following: Quick Barbecue Sauce (below), Mustard-Mayo Sauce (page 206), Chile-Mayo Sauce (page 206), Horseradish Cream (page 54), or Mustard Sauce (page 226).

Makes 8 servings

QUICK BARBECUE SAUCE

As I wrote in *Al Roker's Big Bad Book of Barbecue,* I believe in letting others do as much of the work for me as possible. That's why I like to buy bottled barbecue sauce and doctor it up with a little honey mustard or horseradish. But a lot of folks want to be able to make their own, so I'm including an easy barbecue sauce for those so inclined.

1 tablespoon canola oil, or other vegetable oil
½ onion, peeled and finely chopped
2 cloves garlic, peeled and finely chopped
1 tablespoon chili powder

1 cup ketchup
3 tablespoons cider vinegar
2 tablespoons hot sauce
2 tablespoons frozen orange juice concentrate, thawed

1 • Warm the oil in a saucepan over medium heat. Add the onion and garlic and cook, stirring occasionally, until softened but not browned, about 5 minutes. Add the chili powder and cook, stirring, for 1 minute. Add the ketchup, vinegar, hot sauce, and orange juice, stir well, reduce the heat, cover, and simmer for 15 to 20 minutes, stirring occasionally.
2 • Use the sauce immediately, or cool, cover, and refrigerate for up to 4 days or freeze in an airtight container for up to 2 months (thaw before proceeding). Serve at room temperature or reheat gently and serve hot or warm.

Makes 1½ cups

MUSTARD-MAYO SAUCE

½ cup mayonnaise
½ cup spicy brown mustard
½ cup sour cream

4 teaspoons chopped dill or
  2 teaspoons dried dill, optional
2 teaspoons lemon juice, if using dill

In a small bowl, mix together all of the ingredients. Cover and refrigerate for at least 1 hour and up to 1 week.

Makes 1½ cups

CHILE-MAYO SAUCE

½ cup mayonnaise
½ cup sour cream
¼ cup chopped cilantro leaves

3 tablespoons canned chipotle chile
  peppers in adobo sauce (available in the supermarket), finely
  chopped
2 tablespoons lime juice (from 2 limes)

In a small bowl, mix together all of the ingredients. Cover and refrigerate for at least 1 hour and up to 3 days.

Makes 1½ cups

Grilled Garlic Bread

A great side to go along with the Mixed Grill (page 204), garlic bread is perfect cooked on the grill. The bread gets smoky toasty and the garlic adds just the right bite.

---

6 tablespoons extra-virgin olive oil
6 tablespoons (¾ stick) unsalted
  butter, melted

6 garlic cloves, peeled and finely chopped
¼ teaspoons salt
2 (1-pound) loaves Italian bread

---

1 • In a small bowl, combine the olive oil, butter, garlic, and salt. Let sit for at least 30 minutes and up to 6 hours.

2 • Prepare a charcoal fire or preheat a gas grill for direct grilling over high heat (400°F to 500°F).

3 • Not more than an hour before grilling, cut each loaf in half crosswise and then cut each half in half again lengthwise. You will have 8 pieces of bread. Using a pastry brush, brush the cut side of each piece with the garlic mixture. Use a spoon to distribute a bit of the cut garlic on each piece.

4 • Grill the bread, cut side up, for 1 to 2 minutes. Turn and grill for 1 to 2 minutes more, until well toasted. Watch carefully so that the bread doesn't burn. Serve immediately.

Makes 8 servings

Warm Potato Salad with Bacon

This is not your typical mayonnaise-y potato salad. It's warm, and it's got bacon . . . another way to slip some more meat into the meal. Hey, it's your day, pal!!!

8 slices bacon, diced
1 onion, peeled and cut into ¼-inch pieces
2 cloves garlic, peeled and finely chopped
2 stalks celery, trimmed and cut into ¼-inch pieces
¾ cup chicken broth
⅓ cup cider vinegar
1 teaspoon mustard

3 pounds potatoes, preferably Idaho russets (about 5 medium) or Yukon gold (about 8 medium), peeled and sliced about ½ inch thick
3 large scallions, white and green parts, chopped
2 teaspoons dill seeds, optional
1 large dill pickle, chopped, optional
Salt
Freshly ground pepper

1 • Line a plate with paper towels. Heat a skillet over medium-high heat and, when hot, add the bacon. Cook, stirring occasionally, until crisp, about 10 minutes. Using a slotted spoon, transfer the bacon to the prepared plate to drain. Once cool, the bacon can be covered and kept at room temperature for up to 1 day.

2 • Pour off all but 4 tablespoons of bacon fat from the skillet and return to the stove over medium heat. Add the onion and garlic and cook, stirring, until softened but not browned, about 5 minutes. Stir in the celery and cook for 2 minutes. Stir in the broth, vinegar, and mustard, bring to a boil, reduce the heat, and simmer for a few minutes until the mixture thickens slightly. The dressing can be cooled, covered, and refrigerated for up to 1 day. Reheat gently before tossing with the potatoes.

3 • Pour 2 to 3 inches of water into a large pot and bring to a boil. Set the potatoes in a steamer basket over the boiling water, taking care that the potatoes are not sitting in the water. Cover and steam until they can be easily pierced with a knife, 12 to 15 minutes. Transfer the potatoes to a large serving bowl and let cool slightly.

4 • Toss the dressing with the warm potatoes in the bowl. Sprinkle the scallions, dill seeds, and pickle, if using, over the potatoes and season with salt and pepper. Stir gently to mix, top with the crisp bacon bits, and serve warm or at room temperature.

Makes 8 servings

Cashew Coleslaw

This is an interesting coleslaw. It's tangy, thanks to the sour cream, and it's got a crunchy surprise courtesy of the cashews.

FOR THE DRESSING

¼ cup mayonnaise
¼ cup sour cream
2 teaspoons sugar

¼ teaspoon salt
¼ teaspoon freshly ground pepper

In a small bowl, whisk together all of the ingredients. Cover and refrigerate for at least 30 minutes and up to 2 days.

FOR THE SLAW

¼ large head green cabbage, cored
¼ medium head red cabbage, cored
2 medium carrots, peeled
4 scallions, white and green parts, chopped

½ red or green bell pepper, stemmed, seeded, and chopped
⅔ cup roasted, salted cashews

1 • Using a sharp knife, shred the cabbages (you can also shred them using a food processor). You should have about 5 cups of green cabbage and 4 cups of red cabbage. Grate the carrots in the food processor, or on the largest holes of a box grater.

2 • In a large serving bowl, mix together the cabbage, carrots, scallions, and bell pepper. The mixture can be covered and refrigerated for up to 1 day.

3 • About 30 minutes before serving, toss the coleslaw with the dressing to coat. Just before serving, add the cashews and toss to mix.

Makes 8 servings

Frosted Yellow Cake

For the most part, Dads like uncomplicated desserts. Don't give us froufrou stuff. Make it simple, make it good, and make it now.

FOR THE CAKE

16 tablespoons (2 sticks) unsalted
    butter, softened (page 25)
1½ cups sugar
1 tablespoon pure vanilla extract
3 large eggs
2 cups all-purpose flour
⅓ cup cornstarch

2 teaspoons baking powder
½ teaspoon salt
1 cup whole milk
Red Velvet Cake frosting
    (pages 64–65) or Texas Sheet
    Cake frosting (pages 113–14)

1 • Position a rack in the center of the oven and preheat the oven to 350°F. Lightly butter and flour two 9-inch round cake pans.

2 • Using an electric mixer or mixing by hand, beat together the butter, sugar, and vanilla until light and fluffy, about 3 minutes. Add the eggs, one at a time, beating for about 30 seconds after each addition.

3 • In another bowl, stir together the flour, cornstarch, baking powder, and salt. Gradually stir the dry ingredients into the butter mixture, alternating with the milk, until the ingredients are just incorporated and the batter is smooth. Do not overmix. Using a rubber spatula, scrape the batter evenly into the 2 prepared pans.

4 • Bake the cakes for 30 to 35 minutes, until they just begin to pull away from the sides of the pans and a knife inserted in the center of each comes out clean.

5 • Remove the pans from the oven and place on wire racks to cool for about 15 minutes. Run a knife around the edges of the pans and remove the cakes from the pans by inverting them onto the racks. Turn right side up and let cool thoroughly before frosting. The cakes can be stored, well wrapped, at room temperature for up to 2 days or frozen for up to 2 months (thaw at room temperature before proceeding).

6 • Place 1 cake layer on a serving plate and spread with a little less than half the frosting. Place the remaining cake layer on top and frost the top and sides with the remaining frosting. Serve immediately or let sit at room temperature for up to 6 hours.

Makes one 9-inch layer cake, or about 10 servings

Banana Cream Pie

Why do men like banana cream pie? Because it's the pie of choice in a Three Stooges pie fight. It holds together well in flight, and the graham cracker crust doesn't smother you after impact. And the victim has a big smile on his face after meeting, and eating, his match. Now that's a pie!!!

FOR THE CRUST

1 store-bought (9-inch) graham
    cracker crust
or
1½ cups vanilla wafer crumbs (40 to
    45 wafers)

¼ cup sugar
6 tablespoons (¾ stick) unsalted
    butter, melted

1 • If making the crust, position a rack in the center of the oven. Preheat the oven to 350° F. Generously butter a 9-inch pie plate.

2 • In a medium bowl, mix together the cookie crumbs, sugar, and melted butter. Press into the prepared pie plate. Bake until the crust begins to bubble up, about 8 minutes. Remove from the oven and place on a wire rack to cool completely (the crust must be thoroughly cooled before you proceed).

FOR THE FILLING

4 large egg yolks
½ cup sugar
3 tablespoons cornstarch
½ teaspoon salt
2 cups whole milk

3 tablespoons unsalted butter, cut
    into chunks
2 teaspoons pure vanilla extract
3 ripe medium bananas

1 • In a medium bowl, whisk together the egg yolks, sugar, cornstarch, and salt until thoroughly blended. Set aside.

2 • Fill a large bowl halfway with ice and cold water. Set out a smaller bowl (with a minimum capacity of 1 quart) that will fit inside the larger bowl.

3 • Bring the milk to a gentle boil in a medium saucepan over medium-low heat. Slowly add about ½ cup of the hot milk to the egg mixture, whisking briskly to combine. Stir the yolk mixture into the remaining milk in the saucepan and bring to a gentle boil over medium-high heat, whisking constantly. Continue to cook, whisking, for 2 minutes. The custard should be quite thick. Remove the pan from the heat and whisk in the butter pieces until melted. Add the vanilla and whisk to blend thoroughly.

4 • Pour the custard into the smaller bowl and place the bowl into the ice water bath that you have prepared. Stir to cool the mixture to room temperature.

5 • Peel the bananas and slice them about ¼ inch thick. Place a layer on the bottom of the prepared crust. Pour in half the custard and slice more bananas on top. Finish with the remaining custard, smoothing the top with a flat metal spatula or a butter knife. Cover loosely with plastic wrap and refrigerate for at least 2 hours and up to 8 hours.

FOR THE TOPPING

1 cup heavy cream	*1 teaspoon pure vanilla extract*
2 tablespoons sugar	

1 • Using an electric mixer or whisking by hand, whip the cream until it holds soft peaks. Add the sugar and vanilla and whip until stiff peaks form. Use a pastry bag fitted with a large star tip to pipe the whipped cream in large rosettes all over the pie, or simply spoon the whipped cream over the pie.

2 • Cut the pie into 8 wedges and serve immediately.

Makes one 9-inch pie, or 8 servings

Fourth of July Picnic

Fourth of July is one of those great holidays that has everything going for it. In my family, it usually started with Dad loading the six little Rokers and Mom into the Ford Country Squire station wagon and it ended with fireworks.

Everything in between was mostly about food, with a softball or volleyball game thrown in the mix to attempt to work off the nonstop eating.

For my mother, it was all about the portability of the food. Hermetically sealed containers of mayonnaise-laden potato salad, macaroni salad, and other spoilables were laid in the cooler with dry ice. It was the maternal version of a cryogenic chamber. I think she stored Walt Disney's head in there.

Today, portability is still key. For a Fourth of July picnic, you want foods that travel well AND taste good. So let's get fire-crackin'!

Fizzy Raspberry Lemonade

Fourth of July means lemonade. But let's make it a little interesting shall we? Yeah, you can use those powdered mixes, and they do travel well, but . . . yeeccccchhhh! How about something that doesn't take much longer but tastes like summer is supposed to taste.

3 cups (12 ounces) frozen raspberries
1 quart cold water
About 1 cup sugar
1 cup lemon juice (from 4 to 6 lemons)

2 (12-ounce) cans seltzer (3 cups), chilled
Ice cubes, for serving
1 lemon, halved and sliced, for serving

1 • Using a food processor or blender, puree the raspberries and 2 cups of the water until smooth. Strain through a sieve into a 2-quart pitcher, discarding the raspberry seeds.

2 • Pour the remaining 2 cups water into the food processor or blender. Add 1 cup sugar and blend until dissolved. Add to the pitcher, along with the lemon juice, and stir. Cover and refrigerate until thoroughly chilled, at least 2 hours and up to 3 days.

3 • If taking to a picnic, transport the raspberry lemonade base in an insulated jug and pack the chilled seltzer in a cooler. Just before serving, gently stir the seltzer into the lemonade. Taste and stir in more sugar, if needed. Serve over ice, garnished with lemon slices.

Makes about 2 quarts, or enough for eight 8-ounce servings

Antipasti Salad

It's tasty, it's colorful, and it's quick! And rest easy microbe-hunters . . . it needs no refrigeration. I mean, you can't store it in the cupboard after mixing it, but it'll make it through your picnic.

1 (19-ounce) can cannellini beans, rinsed and drained
3 tablespoons extra-virgin olive oil
1 head roasted garlic (page 27), optional
Salt
Freshly ground pepper
1 (12-ounce) jar roasted red peppers

2 (6-ounce) jars marinated artichoke hearts
1 (6-ounce) jar pitted imported black olives, such as Kalamata olives
2 teaspoons capers, drained
1 (2-ounce) can anchovy fillets packed in oil, optional
1 baguette, sliced

1 • Using a food processor or blender, puree the beans and olive oil until smooth. If using the roasted garlic, squeeze it into the mixture and puree. Season with salt and pepper. The puree can be covered and refrigerated for up to 1 day.

2 • You can bring all the remaining ingredients with you on your picnic in their unopened jars and open and drain them just before serving. Spoon the bean puree in a thick stripe down the center of a serving platter. Lay overlapping slices of red pepper next to the beans on each side, and arrange the artichoke hearts next to the peppers. Scatter the olives and capers on top. Place the anchovies, if using, around the edges.

3 • Serve with the sliced baguette.

Makes 8 servings

Oven-Fried Chicken
with Pecan-Cornmeal Crust

Remember having fried chicken at a Fourth of July picnic? You don't? Well, you need to make some memories. This chicken is so good, it'll make you forget what you had before. But you can't blame this chicken for making you forget where you put the car keys.

*1 (3½- to 4-pound) chicken, cut into
    8 pieces*
2 large eggs
¼ cup whole milk
½ cup finely chopped pecans
⅓ cup cornmeal
⅓ cup all-purpose flour

1 teaspoon salt
1 teaspoon onion powder
½ teaspoon cayenne pepper
½ teaspoon freshly ground pepper
*2 tablespoons unsalted butter, cut
    into small pieces*

1 • Position a rack in the center of the oven, and preheat the oven to 425°F. Using heavy-duty aluminum foil, line a 9 by 13-inch baking dish with sides at least 1½ inches high.

2 • Rinse the chicken under cold running water and pat dry with paper towels.

3 • In a shallow bowl, whisk together the eggs and milk. In another shallow bowl, stir together the pecans, cornmeal, flour, salt, onion powder, cayenne, and pepper.

4 • Dip the chicken pieces into the egg mixture, and then dredge them in the pecan-cornmeal mixture. Place the chicken in the prepared baking dish. Dot with the butter and bake until golden brown, about 1 hour and 15 minutes. The chicken can be cooled, wrapped and refrigerated for up to 24 hours.

5 • Serve hot, at room temperature, or cold.

Makes 4 servings

Vegetarian Picnic Sandwich

We wouldn't want to leave out our vegetarian friends, so here's a nifty sandwich that is easy to prep and tastes great. You can make it the night before and throw it in the picnic basket in the morning. Who says meat lovers and veggie huggers can't get along?

1 (1-pound) loaf Italian bread	*½ small red onion, peeled and thinly*
½ cup sun-dried tomatoes packed	*sliced*
in oil	*4 bottled hot cherry peppers,*
6 ounces whole-milk mozzarella	*stemmed, seeded, and thinly*
cheese, sliced as thinly as possible	*sliced, optional*
Small handful basil leaves (about	*Several leaves romaine or other*
10 leaves)	*sturdy lettuce*

1 • Slice the bread in half lengthwise. Using a pastry brush, brush both halves of the bread with the sun-dried tomato oil.

2 • Arrange the mozzarella on the bottom half of the bread. Top with the basil, sun-dried tomatoes, red onion, hot peppers, if using, lettuce, and, finally, the other half of the bread. Wrap tightly in plastic wrap or aluminum foil. Let sit at room temperature for at least 1 hour and up to 8 hours, or refrigerate overnight. Slice into quarters just before serving.

Makes 4 servings

Classic Macaroni Salad

Look, this is nothing fancy. It's pasta, mayo, and a few other things. It's been around for decades and will be there on picnic tables long after we're gone. Wow, how depressing is that. Okay, forget I said that. Man, this is good macaroni salad. It's basic and tasty. Just be sure it stays in the cooler until you're ready to serve it, and put it back in the cooler after you've finished.

1½ pounds elbow macaroni
8 ounces cubed cheddar cheese (2 cups)
1 green bell pepper, stemmed, seeded,
    and cut into ¼-inch pieces
1 red bell pepper, stemmed, seeded,
    and cut into ¼-inch pieces
½ large red onion, peeled and thinly sliced
6 gherkin pickles, drained and
    chopped (1 cup)

1 (6-ounce) jar green olives stuffed
    with pimientos, drained
½ pound ham, cut into chunks,
    optional
⅔ cup mayonnaise
2 tablespoons cider vinegar
Salt
Freshly ground pepper

1 • Bring a large pot of salted water to a boil and cook the macaroni according to package directions until al dente (cooked but still firm). Drain the macaroni and rinse them under cold running water to stop the cooking. Drain well.

2 • Put the macaroni in a large bowl; add the cheese, bell peppers, onion, gherkins, and olives. Add the ham, if using. Toss to mix. The pasta salad can be covered and refrigerated for up to 24 hours.

3 • If transporting to a picnic, pack the salad in a covered, plastic bowl or a large plastic freezer bag, and keep in a cooler until ready to serve. Combine the mayonnaise and vinegar in a separate container, cover, and store in the cooler.

4 • Within an hour of serving, toss the salad with the mayonnaise and vinegar and season with salt and pepper.

Makes 8 servings

Three-Bean Salad

I like the crunch of the green beans, the creaminess of the chickpeas and the earthiness of the kidney bean. Three beans, one fab salad.

½ pound green beans or yellow wax beans, or a combination, into 1-inch lengths

1 (19-ounce) can kidney beans, rinsed and drained

1 (19-ounce) can chickpeas, rinsed and drained

¼ cup extra-virgin olive oil

1 medium onion, peeled and cut into ¼-inch pieces

2 cloves garlic, peeled and finely chopped

2 tablespoons all-purpose flour

½ cup cider vinegar

½ cup chicken broth

3 tablespoons sugar

1 teaspoon dry mustard

½ teaspoon hot red pepper flakes

2 stalks celery, trimmed and cut into ¼-inch pieces

1 red bell pepper, stemmed, seeded, and cut into ¼-inch pieces

Salt

Freshly ground pepper

1 • Bring a medium pot of salted water to a boil, add the green beans, and cook until just tender but still bright green, 4 to 6 minutes. Drain the beans and run them under cold water to stop the cooking. Transfer to a bowl and add the kidney beans and chickpeas. Toss to combine.

2 • Warm the oil in a saucepan over medium heat. Add the onion and garlic and cook, stirring, until softened but not browned, about 5 minutes. Sprinkle in the flour and cook, stirring, for 2 to 3 minutes. Add the vinegar, chicken broth, sugar, mustard, and red pepper flakes. Simmer, stirring, until quite thick, about 4 minutes. Add the celery and bell pepper and cook just until slightly softened, about 2 minutes. Season with salt and pepper.

3 • Stir the dressing into the beans and let cool. Cover and refrigerate the salad for at least 2 hours to blend the flavors, or up to 2 days.

Makes 8 servings

Platinum Blondies

Sometimes I feel like having a brownie, but I'm not in the mood for chocolate. These fit the bill and will get gobbled up at your picinic. Kids can grab 'em and go. For that matter, so can adults. So make sure you stash a couple or you may end up empty-handed at your own picnic.

¾ cup plus 2 tablespoons packed light brown sugar	*½ teaspoon baking soda*
1 large egg	*⅛ teaspoon salt*
2 teaspoons vanilla extract	*1 cup chopped pecans, toasted (page 23)*
8 tablespoons (1 stick) unsalted butter, melted	*4 ounces white chocolate, chopped, or ¾ cup white chocolate chips*
¾ cup all-purpose flour	

1 • Position a rack in the center of the oven and preheat the oven to 325°F. Lightly butter an 8-inch square baking pan with sides at least 1½ inches high.

2 • Using an electric mixer or mixing by hand, beat together the sugar and egg until light and fluffy, about 3 minutes. Add the vanilla and butter and beat to mix well. In a small bowl, stir together the flour, baking soda, and salt and add to the butter mixture, beating until just incorporated. Do not overmix. Using a spoon, stir in the pecans and white chocolate. Spoon the batter into the prepared pan and use a flat metal spatula or a butter knife to smooth the top.

3 • Bake the blondies for 25 to 30 minutes, until the top is dry and golden and a knife inserted in the center comes out with just a few crumbs attached (not wet, but not perfectly dry). Remove the pan from the oven and place on a wire rack to cool. Cut the blondies into 2-inch squares. The blondies can be stored, well wrapped, at room temperature for up to 3 days (these seem to get better as they sit) or frozen for up to 2 months (thaw before serving).

Makes sixteen 2-inch squares

Candy Bar Bars

You know why I love this recipe. It is perfect on a hot July afternoon. Here's the deal. First, they taste great. But what makes 'em fabulous for your picnic is that you can freeze them ahead of time, letting them thaw during the picnic. By the time you're ready to serve dessert, they're soft enough to eat. They're a terrific warm-weather surprise.

8 tablespoons (1 stick) unsalted
    butter, softened (page 25)
1¼ cups sugar
3 large eggs
2 teaspoons vanilla extract
1¼ cups all-purpose flour

6 tablespoons unsweetened cocoa
    powder
½ teaspoon baking powder
¼ teaspoon salt
4 (2.07-ounce) peanut-and-caramel
    chocolate candy bars, cut into
    ¼-inch pieces

1 • Position a rack in the center of the oven and preheat the oven to 350°F. Lightly butter an 8-inch square baking pan with sides at least 1½ inches high.

2 • Using an electric mixer or mixing by hand, beat together the butter, sugar, eggs, and vanilla until light and fluffy, about 3 minutes. In a small bowl, stir together the flour, cocoa powder, baking powder, and salt and add to the butter mixture, beating only until the batter is a uniform color. Do not overmix. Using a spoon, stir in the candy bar pieces. Spoon the batter into the prepared pan and use a flat metal spatula or a butter knife to smooth the top.

3 • Bake the bars for 35 to 40 minutes, until a knife inserted in the center comes out with just a few crumbs attached (not wet, but not perfectly dry). Remove the pan from the oven and place on a wire rack to cool. Cut the bars into 2-inch squares. The bars can be stored, well wrapped, at room temperature for up to 3 days or frozen for up to 2 months (thaw before serving).

Makes sixteen 2-inch squares

St. Lawrence Day Barbecue (August 10th)

Who knew there was a patron saint of barbecue? Well, once you hear his story, you'll agree not only is he the patron saint, he's got a heck of a sense of humor.

These days, Lawrence is the man who gets to lead a suffering soul out of Purgatory and into heaven. This pleasant job is his reward for the suffering he endured because of his faith and because of his tweaking of a Roman Emperor.

According to the book *Saints Preserve Us* by Sean Kelly and Rosemary Rogers, around 200 A.D., Lawrence was the treasurer of the Church of Rome. As such, he was the keeper of the cash and assets. When Roman authorities arrested the Pope, the Pope told Lawrence to gather the Church's wealth and distribute it to the poor, so that it would not fall into the hands of the Roman authorities.

When the Romans got wind of this, they gave Lawrence three days to show up at the Roman prefect's palace with the Church's booty. But Lawrence wouldn't give up without a fight. When he showed up at the Roman prefect's palace door, he had thousands of lepers, widows, homeless, and disabled with him. St. Lawrence announced, "This is the Church's treasure."

As you might imagine, the prefect didn't see the humor in his gesture and had Lawrence tortured. At one point, he was placed on a rack and literally roasted over a fire. Legend has it Lawrence turned to his tormentors and said, "Turn me over, I'm done on this side." Now *that* is a patron saint of barbecue.

Smoked Beef Ribs with Mustard Sauce

When you think of barbecue, some of you think of pork. But depending on where you're from, barbecue could just as easily mean beef. This recipe shows you how to smoke the beef for the best flavor. It may take a little time to prep the short ribs, but they're worth it.

3/4 cup mustard
6 tablespoons canola or other
    vegetable oil
6 tablespoons packed light brown
    sugar
6 tablespoons orange juice

1 teaspoon onion powder
Freshly ground pepper
6 pounds beef ribs (see note)
Coarse salt
About 2 cups wood chips (hickory,
    oak, or apple)

---

1 • In a small bowl, stir together the mustard, oil, brown sugar, orange juice, onion powder, and ¼ teaspoon pepper. Let sit for at least 30 minutes, or cover and refrigerate for up to 3 days. Set aside ½ cup of the sauce for basting, and reserve the rest for serving with the cooked ribs.

2 • Rinse the ribs under cold running water and pat them dry with paper towels. Sprinkle with salt and pepper. Let sit at room temperature for 30 minutes before grilling.

3 • Soak the wood chips for at least 30 minutes in cold water. Prepare a charcoal fire or preheat a gas grill for indirect grilling over low heat (250°F to 300°F). Drain the wood chips and add 1 cup to the grill.

4 • Cook the ribs, with the grill covered, for 1½ hours, without turning. Don't forget to add more wood chips—and, if using charcoal, more coals—as needed (check after 1 hour).

5 • Turn the ribs over and, using a barbecue mop (available in kitchen stores), a pastry brush, or a long-handled spoon, generously baste the ribs using the reserved ½ cup barbecue sauce. Grill for 30 minutes longer, then turn and baste again with the sauce. Grill for about 10 to 15 more minutes, until the ribs are dark brown and the meat has shrunk back from the bones.

6 • If the ribs are done before you are ready to eat, wrap them in heavy-duty aluminum foil and leave them over very low, indirect heat for up to 1 hour.

7 • Serve with the reserved barbecue sauce on the side.

Makes 4 main-course servings, or 8 appetizer servings

NOTE: These are sold as "flat ribs," usually in a 2½- to 3-pound rack. If they have already been cut into individual ribs, that's okay. Six pounds (2 racks) of ribs is about all that will fit on the average grill. If you want to do more, borrow a grill or invite a friend to bring one.

Texas Brisket

If you like beef, and have never had barbecued beef brisket, you are in for a treat. When it's done right, it is tender, succulent, and smoky. You might compare it to a religious experience. Say Amen and Hallelujah! You will light a candle at the altar of St. Lawrence.

3 tablespoons chili powder
3 tablespoons sugar
2 tablespoons sweet paprika
1 tablespoon garlic powder
2 teaspoons onion powder
1 teaspoon ground cumin
1 tablespoon salt
1 teaspoon freshly ground black pepper
1/4 teaspoon cayenne pepper

1 brisket (5 to 6 pounds) (see note)
About 5 cups wood chips (hickory, oak or apple)
1/2 cup canola oil or other vegetable oil
1/4 cup cider vinegar
2 tablespoons honey
1 (14-ounce) can beef broth
1 (12-ounce) bottle beer

1 • In a small bowl, stir together the chili powder, sugar, paprika, garlic powder, onion powder, cumin, salt, black pepper, and cayenne. The spice rub can be covered and stored at room temperature for up to 6 months.

2 • Rinse the meat under cold running water and pat dry with paper towels. Set aside 2 tablespoons of the rub to make the mop sauce. Pat the remaining rub all over the brisket on both sides, rubbing it in with your hands. Cover with plastic wrap and refrigerate for at least 8 hours and up to 24 hours. Let sit at room temperature for about 30 minutes before grilling.

3 • Soak the wood chips for at least 30 minutes in cold water.

4 • In a bowl, combine the oil, vinegar, and honey, stirring well to dissolve the honey as much as possible. Stir in the reserved 2 tablespoons spice rub to make the mop sauce for basting.

5 • Pour the beef broth and beer into a disposable 9 by 13-inch aluminum pan with sides at least 1½ inches high. Place the pan in the center of the grill, under the grilling grate. (The brisket will sit on the grate, over this pan. The pan will catch the drippings, and the liquid in the pan will flavor the meat and keep it moist.)

6 • Prepare a charcoal fire or preheat a gas grill for indirect grilling over very low heat (225°F to 250°F). Drain the wood chips and add 1 cup to the grill.

7 • Put the brisket, fat side up, on the grill, over the pan. Using a barbecue mop (available in kitchen stores), a pastry brush, or a long-handled spoon, coat the brisket with the mop sauce. Grill the brisket, with the grill covered, basting with the mop every hour and turning once, until a meat thermometer or an instant-read thermometer inserted in the thickest part of the meat registers 190°F. This will take 4½ to 6 hours, depending on the size of the brisket, and the heat of your grill. Don't forget to add more wood chips and—if using charcoal, more coals—as needed (check every hour or so). You should have enough soaked wood chips for about 5 hours of cooking time; if the brisket takes longer, you will need to soak more chips.

8 • Remove the brisket from the grill and place it on a cutting board. Cover the meat with a piece of aluminum foil to keep it warm and let it rest for at least 5 minutes before slicing. Slice the meat thinly, against the grain (otherwise it will be tough). Serve as-is, or with Quick Barbecue Sauce (page 205) on the side. (Never insult a brisket aficionado by slathering the cooked meat with sauce.)

Makes 10 to 12 servings

NOTE: Ideally, you want to buy a brisket with a thick layer of fat on top. If you can't buy a 6-pounder, buy two 3- to 4-pounders. The method and cooking time remain the same.

Braised Greens and Turnips

Since we're in the church of St. Lawrence, let us genuflect and reflect on a great side dish for a barbecue: greens. In most churches, you're supposed to leave something in the plate. In the Church of St. Lawrence, your plate should be clean when you leave. Y'all come back and try these out, y'heah.

4 to 5 pounds medium turnips with turnip greens (see note)
½ pound salt pork, cut into 4 chunks
2 cups water

½ teaspoon hot red pepper flakes
Salt
Freshly ground pepper

1 • Cut the greens off the turnips and cut off and discard any thick, tough stems from the greens. Rinse the leaves well, drain them, and put them in a bowl of cold water. Peel the turnips and cut them into ¾-inch pieces. Set aside.

2 • Cook the salt pork in a heavy saucepan over medium-high heat until the bottom of the pot is coated with about 2 tablespoons of fat. Using a slotted spoon, remove the salt pork from the pot and set it aside.

3 • Drain the greens quickly in a colander, leaving some water still on the leaves. Place them in the hot pan. Cover and cook until wilted, about 10 minutes.

4 • Add the water, turnips, red pepper flakes, and the reserved salt pork. Stir to mix well. Reduce the heat, cover, and simmer for 20 to 30 minutes, or until the leaves are tender and the turnips can be easily pierced with a knife. Season with salt and pepper. The turnips and greens can be cooled, covered, and refrigerated for up to 24 hours. Reheat gently. Before serving, discard the salt pork.

Makes 8 servings

NOTE: If you buy the greens and turnips separately, you will want about 2 pounds of greens and 6 medium turnips. If you can't find turnip greens, simply substitute collard greens.

VARIATION

Vegetarian Greens and Turnips

Omit the salt pork and use 2 tablespoons canola or other vegetable oil instead to wilt the greens. For added flavor, substitute one 14-ounce can vegetable broth for the water.

Spicy Baked Beans

In *Al Roker's Big Bad Book of Barbecue*, we have a recipe for baked beans. Well, what barbecue would be complete without a recipe for baked beans? Not wanting to repeat myself, I decided it was time to ramp up the amps. Add a little spice to the nice. And as St. Lawrence would say, "Let's bring a little fire to your choir." Okay, I'll stop now, but you get the idea.

1½ pounds dried Navy beans, picked over and rinsed
1 medium onion, peeled and cut into ¼-inch pieces
1 cup Quick Barbecue Sauce (page 205) or store-bought barbecue sauce
1 (4-ounce) can mild or spicy green chiles, drained and finely chopped
½ cup pure maple syrup
1 tablespoon Worcestershire sauce
1 smoked ham hock
1 (14-ounce) can chicken broth, plus additional broth or water if needed

1 • Put the beans in a large pot and add enough cold water to cover by 2 inches. Soak the beans overnight.

2 • If you forgot to soak the beans overnight or don't have time, use the quick-soak method: Bring the beans and water to cover to a boil. Boil for two minutes, shut off the heat, and let the beans sit for 1 hour. Proceed with the recipe.

3 • Drain the beans and return them to the pot. Add enough cold water to cover by 2 inches. Cover the pot, set it over high heat, and bring the water to a boil. Reduce the heat, cover, and simmer until the beans are tender, 45 minutes to 1 hour. Drain the beans.

4 • Position a rack in the center of the oven and preheat the oven to 300°F.

5 • Put the beans in a large, ovenproof pot and stir in the onion, barbecue sauce, chiles, maple syrup, and Worcestershire sauce. Nestle the ham hock in the center of the beans. Add just enough chicken broth so that you can see it seeping through the top of the beans. Cover and bake for 2 hours.

6 • Remove the cover, reduce the heat to 250°F, and bake for an additional 2 to 3 hours, or until the beans are tender and nicely colored. If the beans seem to be drying out, add more chicken broth or some water, as needed.

7 • Remove the ham hock, shred the meat off the bone, and add it to the beans. The beans can be cooled, covered, and refrigerated for up to 2 days or frozen, well wrapped, for up to 2 months (thaw and reheat on the stovetop, adding a bit of broth or water if the beans seem dry, before serving).

Makes 8 servings

Rice Salad with Broccoli and Peanuts

Rice is nice, but a rice salad brings the worlds of starch and veggies together. For those who have been waiting for the greatest combo since the guy with the chocolate bumped into the fella with the peanut butter, St. Lawrence has answered your prayers.

2 cups white rice, or 1 cup white rice and 1 cup brown rice
½ cup olive oil
⅓ cup balsamic vinegar
2 teaspoons finely grated lemon zest (from 1 lemon)
2 tablespoons lemon juice (from 1 lemon)
Salt
Freshly ground pepper

Florets from 1 bunch broccoli, cut into bite-size pieces (about 5 cups)
1 green, red, or yellow bell pepper, stemmed, seeded, and cut into ¼-inch pieces
4 large scallions, white and green parts, chopped
2 cups cherry or grape tomatoes, stemmed and halved
1 cup unsalted, roasted peanuts
1 cup chopped parsley leaves

1 • Cook the rice according to package directions. (If using both brown and white rice, cook each in a separate pot since brown rice takes longer to cook). Rinse the rice under cold running water to remove some of the starch and drain well. Spoon the rice into a large bowl and add the oil, vinegar, lemon zest, and lemon juice. Season with salt and pepper and stir to combine.

2 • Bring a small pot of salted water to a boil, add the broccoli, and cook until just tender but still very green, about 4 minutes. Drain and run under cold water to stop the cooking. Drain well and add to the rice.

3 • Stir in the bell pepper, scallions, tomatoes, peanuts, and parsley.

4 • The salad is best served the day it is made, but can be kept, covered and refrigerated, for up to 24 hours. Serve cold or at room temperature.

Makes 8 servings

Chopped Summer Salad

The Lord has provided a bounty of fresh summer vegetables. In honor of the Feast of St. Lawrence, we offer this salad that celebrates this great plenty. Your parishioners will eat it fast, so get to it . . . chop-chop.

2 large ears corn, husked
2 small zucchini, trimmed and cut
    into ¼-inch pieces
1 yellow summer squash, cut into
    ¼-inch pieces
2 cups cherry or grape tomatoes,
    stemmed and halved

½ medium red onion, peeled and
    thinly sliced
3 tablespoons extra-virgin olive oil
2 tablespoons lemon juice (from 1 lemon)
Salt
Freshly ground pepper
¼ cup chopped basil leaves
½ cup chopped parsley leaves

1 • Prepare a charcoal or gas grill for direct cooking over high heat (400°F to 500°F), or bring a few inches of water to boil in a pot.

2 • Grill the corn, turning occasionally, for 8 to 12 minutes, until the kernels look toasty and a few are dark brown. Alternatively, cook the corn in the boiling water for about 5 minutes, until the kernels are tender.

3 • When cool enough to handle, slice the fat end of each cob so it's flat and the ear can stand upright in a bowl. Using a sharp knife, cut the corn off the cob. You should have about 2 cups of kernels.

4 • Combine the corn, zucchini, summer squash, tomatoes, and red onion in a serving bowl. Sprinkle with the oil and lemon juice and season with salt and pepper. Add the basil and parsley to the bowl and toss well to combine. Let the salad sit at room temperature for at least for 30 minutes to blend the flavors, or cover and refrigerate for up to 8 hours.

5 • Serve chilled or at room temperature.

Makes 8 servings

Grilled Glazed Doughnuts with Vanilla Ice Cream

This is one recipe for which I can thank Deborah and, indirectly, my son Nicholas. We had just finished some grilled lamb chops, and I was cleaning the grill. Deborah, who was near her due date for Nicholas, was still ravenous. She really wanted something sweet.

I had taken some ice cream out to temper, figuring that would be dessert. Out of the blue, I got an idea. I had brought home some glazed doughnuts earlier in the day. Glazed doughnuts are sooooo good when they've just come off the conveyor belt piping hot, right? I turned the grill back up, grabbed two doughnuts, sliced them in half, and put 'em on.

Within a minute, the doughnuts had grill marks on each side and were nice and crunchy. I put one half on a plate, then a scoop of the ice cream, and the other half on top.

Talk about deliverance. I hate to say it when we're celebrating the Feast of St. Lawrence, but . . . it's sinfully good.

8 glazed doughnuts, halved lengthwise	*1 pint vanilla ice cream*

1 • Prepare a charcoal fire or preheat a gas grill for direct grilling over high (400°F to 500°F).

2 • Place the doughnuts on the grill and grill for 30 seconds per side, until toasted. Serve immediately with a scoop of ice cream in between each 2 halves.

Makes 8 servings

Labor Day
Summer Send-Off

Labor Day is one of those holidays that's sort of lost its meaning. It's a celebration of the strides that the organized Labor movement has made in this country. I remember my Dad marching in the Labor Day parade, along with the other members of the Transport Workers Union. As the family of a bus driver, we reaped the advantages fought for by those who worked so hard to get the working stiff the pay and benefits he deserved, including holidays off. So to celebrate labor, we don't labor.

When I was a kid, Labor Day seemed like a bit of a waste. We were already off from school, so what was the point? And of course, Labor Day meant that school was, in fact, not just around the corner. It was at your front door, looking through the curtains in your living room window, saying, "It's me, Mr. School. I'm coming for you . . . a couple of days, Sparky, and you're mine . . . all mine!!!!"

I always hate to see Labor Day show up. He's the Summer Party Pooper. All the fun, the warm weather, the swimming, the backyard barbecues are toast. Okay, technically you can still do some of that stuff after Labor Day; summer is still on the books until late September. But it's not the same.

When you were a kid in school, the difference between Friday and Saturday was humongous. Friday, you'd have the whole weekend ahead of you. The possibilities were endless. Saturday, half the weekend was already gone. Your fun was, for all intents and purposes, over. And Sunday . . . fuggedaboudit. You may as well have gone to school on Sunday. Well, Labor Day is the Sunday of summer.

But let's send summer out with a bang. Let's have a great Labor Day. With help from these recipes, you will say, "So long, summer" with a smile and a tire iron secreted behind your back for "Mr. School."

Ham and Pineapple Appetizers

What better way to keep summer in your heart than to have a luau in your mouth. Think Don Ho dancing on your tongue. Ewwwwwwwww.

1 fresh pineapple	1/3 pound thinly sliced ham

1 • Soak wooden toothpicks or skewers in water for at least 5 minutes to prevent them from burning.

2 • Using a large, sharp knife, trim off the crown and tough bottom part of the pineapple and discard. Stand the pineapple upright and slice off the tough outer skin. Cut the pineapple flesh crosswise into 3/4-inch-thick slices. Cut each slice in half and cut out the core. Cut each half slice into 3 or 4 chunks.

3 • Cut the ham slices into 1-inch strips. Wrap 1 strip around each pineapple chunk and secure with a toothpick. You can also spear 3 chunks on a wooden skewer. Place the skewered ham-wrapped pineapple on a baking sheet until ready to grill or broil. The skewers can be covered and refrigerated for up to 24 hours.

4 • Prepare a charcoal fire or preheat a gas grill for direct grilling over high heat (400°F to 500°F), or position a rack so that it is 4 to 5 inches from the heat source of the broiler and preheat the broiler.

5 • If grilling, put the ham-pineapple chunks directly on the grill. If broiling, leave them on the baking sheet. Grill or broil for 5 minutes. Turn and cook for 3 to 4 minutes longer, until fragrant and beginning to brown. Arrange on a warm platter and serve immediately.

Makes at least 36 pieces, or 12 skewers

Orange Beef Tidbits

In keeping with our semitropical theme, here's a little beefy something that'll make you say, "Book 'em, Dan-O."

¼ cup soy sauce
2 cloves garlic, peeled and finely chopped
1 tablespoon peeled, chopped fresh ginger
1 tablespoon finely grated orange zest (from 1 orange)

1 tablespoon orange juice (from 1 orange)
1 tablespoon canola oil, or other vegetable oil
2 teaspoons sugar
½ teaspoon hot red pepper flakes
1½ pounds beef sirloin, cut into 1½-inch chunks

---

1 • Add all of the ingredients except the beef to a shallow bowl or pan and stir to mix well. Add the beef and toss to coat. Cover and refrigerate for at least 8 hours and up to 24 hours, turning the meat once.

2 • Prepare a charcoal fire or preheat a gas grill for direct grilling over high heat (400°F to 500°F), or position a rack so that it is 4 to 5 inches from the heat source of the broiler and preheat the broiler.

3 • Soak wooden toothpicks or skewers in water for at least 5 minutes to prevent them from burning. Remove the beef tidbits from the marinade and skewer them on the toothpicks, discarding the marinade. You can also spear 3 pieces of beef on a skewer. Place the skewered beef on a rimmed baking sheet.

4 • If grilling, put the beef chunks directly on the grill. If broiling, leave them on the baking sheet. Grill or broil the beef 4 to 6 minutes, turning halfway. Test for doneness by transferring 1 piece to a cutting board and slicing it in half. If not done to your liking, grill or broil some more, checking at 1-minute intervals.

5 • Arrange the skewers on a warm platter and serve immediately.

Makes 36 pieces, or 12 skewers

Curried Chicken Skewers

Maybe you should try kissing up to summer. Then he wouldn't go. How about currying favor with this recipe? Get it? Curry favor . . . curried chicken . . . all right, I'm upset about summer leaving, so my stuff's a little shaky.

½ cup plain yogurt
2 tablespoons mango chutney, plus
    extra for dipping, if desired
2 teaspoons curry powder

2 teaspoons lemon juice
¼ teaspoon salt
1½ pounds boneless, skinless, chicken
    breasts, cut into 1½-inch pieces

1 • In a shallow bowl, stir together the yogurt, chutney, curry powder, lemon juice, and salt. Add the chicken pieces and toss well to coat. Cover and refrigerate for at least 1 hour and up to 8 hours, turning once.

2 • Prepare a charcoal fire or preheat a gas grill for direct grilling over high heat (400°F to 500°F), or position a rack so that it is 4 to 5 inches from the heat source of the broiler and preheat the broiler.

3 • Soak wooden toothpicks or skewers in water for at least 5 minutes to prevent them from burning. Remove the chicken from the marinade and skewer them on the toothpicks, discarding the marinade. You can also spear 3 pieces of chicken on a skewer. Place the skewered chicken on a rimmed baking sheet.

4 • If grilling, put the chicken directly on the grill. If broiling, leave them on the baking sheet. Grill or broil the chicken 4 to 6 minutes, turning halfway. Test for doneness by transferring 1 piece to a cutting board and slicing it in half. If still pink in the middle, grill or broil some more, testing at 1-minute intervals.

5 • Arrange the skewers on a warm platter and serve immediately, with extra chutney for dipping, if desired.

Makes 36 pieces, or 12 skewers

Stovetop Clambake

Since you don't want anymore tropical jokes, let's try a different tack. You tack when you sail. Sailing is big in New England. Clambakes are popular there in the summer . . . I got it!!! A clambake! And you don't even have to get sand in your boat shoes.

---

4 pounds small red potatoes (2½-inch diameter), scrubbed but not peeled
6 pounds littleneck clams or other small to medium clams

8 (1- to 1¼-pound) live lobsters
8 large ears corn, husked
4 lemons, cut into wedges
1 pound (4 sticks) unsalted butter, melted

---

1 • Put the potatoes in a large pot with enough cold water to cover by about 1 inch. Salt the water. Cover the pot and bring to a boil, then reduce the heat and simmer the potatoes for 8 to 10 minutes, until you can just barely pierce them with a knife. Do not overcook; the potatoes will finish cooking later with the seafood. Drain and set aside.

2 • Scrub the clams under cold running water. Discard any that are cracked or open.

3 • Lay out cheesecloth (available in supermarkets) on a flat work surface and cut 5 double-layered, 12-inch squares. Put half of the potatoes in 1 double-layer square, and use the corners to tie a neat packet. Set it aside. Repeat with the remaining potatoes. Divide the clams into 3 equal piles and wrap each pile in each of the remaining cheesecloth squares, as you did the potatoes. Tie and set aside.

4 • The idea is to use 2 pots: 1 really big pot and 1 more regular-size big pot. A 21.5-quart speckled canning pot works perfectly; you can buy one at cookware or hardware stores. It comes with a jar rack; place a round wire cake rack over the top of the jar rack in the pot to create a makeshift steamer basket. The second pot should be an average pasta-cooking pot, and hold about 8 quarts. You need a steamer basket for it, as well.

5 • Bring about 4 inches of water to boil in the bigger pot, and about 3 inches in the other pot. Turn off the heat.

6 • You can arrange the food in the pots any way you like, but the idea is to mix the seafood

with the potatoes and corn so they are all nicely flavored. The following arrangement works well: In the really big pot, place 6 lobsters, 2 packets of clams, and 1 packet of potatoes. In the smaller pot, place 2 lobsters, 1 packet of clams, and 1 packet of potatoes. Cover the pots and bring the water in each back to a boil. Steam for 10 to 12 minutes, then add the corn (6 ears to the big pot, 2 to the smaller one) and steam for about 8 minutes longer, until the lobsters are bright red and the clams have opened.

7 • Using tongs, remove the corn, the packets of potatoes and clams, and the lobsters from the pot. Put each lobster on a cutting board and, using a cleaver or very sharp, heavy-duty knife, cut lengthwise through the middle of the underside of each lobster tail. Cut each claw horizontally across the middle. This will make the meat easier to remove. Put the lobsters on a large platter and surround them with the lemon wedges.

8 • Cut open the cheesecloth packets and discard the cheesecloth, putting the clams and potatoes in large bowls. Discard any clams that have not opened. Divide the melted butter into 8 small bowls. You can squeeze some lemon into the butter if you'd like.

9 • Serve immediately, making sure you have some nut crackers on hand for getting at hard-to-open parts of the lobster.

Makes 8 servings

NOTE: Ask the folks at the fish counter if they have any rockweed —a seaweed that is often shipped with lobster—and, if they do, bring some home and add it to the pot on top of the other ingredients. It's not necessary, but it adds a nice flavor. Discard before serving.

Berry Crisp

I love, love, love, love, loooooooooove berries, and I love, love, love, love, love, love, love, love, love, berry crisp. It is the quintessential summertime dessert. Therefore, it makes perfect sense to serve it at a Labor Day picnic.

FOR THE TOPPING

*½ cup old-fashioned rolled oats
    (not quick-cooking or instant)*
½ cup all-purpose flour
½ cup packed light brown sugar
Pinch of salt

*4 tablespoons unsalted butter, cut
    into small pieces*
*½ cup sliced almonds, toasted
    (page 23)*

In a bowl, stir together the oats, flour, brown sugar, and salt. Using your fingers, rub the butter into the dry ingredients until the mixture resembles crumbs. Mix in the almonds. The topping can be covered and refrigerated for up to 2 days (return to room temperature, and crumble any big clumps, if needed, before proceeding).

FOR THE FILLING

*6 cups whole or sliced berries,
    such as strawberries, blueberries,
    blackberries, or raspberries, or a
    combination*

*4 teaspoons finely grated orange zest
    (from 2 oranges)*
2 tablespoons sugar
*2 tablespoons orange-flavored liqueur
    or orange juice*

1 • Rinse the berries in a colander under cold running water and drain well. If using strawberries, hull them and cut them in half if they are large. In a large bowl, toss the berries with the orange zest, sugar, and liqueur. The berries can be covered and refrigerated for up to 24 hours.

2 • Position a rack in the middle of the oven and preheat the oven to 375°F. Lightly butter a 9-inch pie plate.

3 • Spoon the berry filling into the prepared pie plate. Sprinkle the topping over the fruit. The crisp can be frozen, well wrapped, for up to 1 month.

4 • Put the pie plate on a baking sheet to catch any drips and bake for 45 minutes (about 5 minutes longer if frozen), until the fruit is bubbling and the topping is beginning to brown. Remove from the oven, place on a wire rack, and let cool at least partially.

5 • Serve the crisp warm or at room temperature, scooping out 8 servings into shallow bowls, and topping each serving with whipped cream or ice cream, if desired.

Makes one 9-inch crisp, or 8 servings

Triple Melon Salad

How often does a cookbook give you the opportunity to walk into the grocery store and say, "Nice melons. Can I have those for a salad?"

1 ripe honeydew melon (about
    4½ pounds)
1 ripe cantaloupe (about 3 pounds)
¼ of a large ripe watermelon (about
    4 pounds)
1 tablespoon finely grated lemon zest
    (from 1 lemon)
2 teaspoons finely grated lime zest
    (from 1 lime)

¼ cup chopped mint leaves, plus
    extra whole mint leaves for
    serving
¼ cup sugar
3 tablespoons lemon juice (from
    1 lemon)
3 tablespoons lime juice (from 1 or
    2 limes)

1 • Cut the honeydew and cantaloupe in half and remove the seeds and stringy pulp. Using a melon ball scoop, remove the pulp (you can also just use a knife and cut it into chunks). Do the same with the watermelon pulp, avoiding the seeds. Put all of the fruit into a serving bowl—a glass bowl shows off the colors. Add the lemon and lime zests and chopped mint.

2 • In a small bowl or jar, combine the sugar, lemon juice, and lime juice and stir or shake until the sugar is dissolved. Pour over the fruit salad and toss. Serve immediately or cover and refrigerate for up to 4 hours.

3 • Serve garnished with whole fresh mint leaves.

Makes 8 servings

Halloween Party
for Kids and Grown-Ups

I remember a Halloween party I went to when I was in third grade at P.S. 272. These were the days before they actually gave elementary schools names in New York City. It was like there were too many schools and nobody had time for names. Somebody at the Board of Education in the early 1900s must have said, "Just give 'em numbers! We gotta look up dead people to name the schools after. Who needs the hassle?" I digress.

So there was this Halloween party. It was at the apartment of a girl named Janice. I had a huge crush on her and wanted to win the bobbing for apples contest to impress her.

It was my turn. Just as my face hit the water, I had to sneeze, and I inhaled all this water. I started choking and sneezed into the tub filled with water. Needless to say, no one wanted to bob for apples after that. I don't know if I impressed her, but the look on her face told me she wasn't going to forget me for a while. Although, now that I think about it, I never got another party invite from her. Hmmmmmm.

Nobody seems to give Halloween parties anymore. Sure, they have one at your kids' school, but what with kids and peanut allergies and every other kind of allergy and dietary restriction, they seem to be on the wane.

It's time to bring back the Halloween party. Bring it back big time. Fun time. Not the cheesy Halloween parties you go to as adults. Do we really need to see another forty-something-year-old dressed as Catwoman? I think not.

I'm talkin' really fun, kids' Halloween parties that also have good stuff for the parents or caregivers who will be there with all the little Spidermen, Wonder Women, and Incredible Hulks.

At the Halloween party, you can keep an eye on the little ones and make sure you know what they're eating and how much. Plus they don't have to endure the same angst and humiliation that Charlie Brown did on that infamous night of Trick or Treating.

Third grade may have been the end of my bobbing-for-apples career, but I haven't lost my enthusiasm for a great Halloween party. Try some of these recipes and you'll never get a rock in your Trick or Treat bag.

Cider Punch

It's better than juice boxes and adults and kids will think it's scarrrrry good.

---

2 quarts apple cider, chilled
1 (750 milliliter) bottle sparkling apple
   cider, chilled (about 3½ cups)

2 cups cranberry juice, chilled
Ice cubes, for serving

Just before serving, mix the apple ciders and cranberry juice together in a punch bowl. Add ice cubes and serve.

Makes about 3½ quarts, or about eighteen 6-ounce servings

NOTE: For a ghoulish touch, fill a clean, clear or white plastic glove with water, tie the end tightly, and freeze. Float this ghostly hand in the punch bowl.

Dill Dip

If you want to get the kids to go for it, call it something like Slime Slop or Ghoul Gunk. They will devour it like crazy.

1½ cups sour cream	*3 cloves garlic, peeled and finely*
6 ounces cream cheese, softened	*chopped*
(¾ cup)	*1 tablespoon dried dill*

1 • Using a food processor or blender, combine all of the ingredients and puree until smooth. Spoon into a serving bowl, cover, and refrigerate for at least 1 hour, to blend the flavors, or for up to 2 days.

2 • Serve with sliced raw vegetables and/or bagel chips for dipping.

Makes about 2 cups

NOTE: You can serve the dip in several carved-out mini pumpkins, or carve out just enough of a small pumpkin to hold a 2-cup serving bowl.

Mini Burgers

For your Halloween party, how about calling these Mini Alien Attack Ships? No? All right, Mini Monster Toenails in Baby Buns? Whatever you call 'em, call 'em gone, 'cause these are really good.

1¼ pounds ground beef, pork, or
    turkey, or a combination
1 large egg
½ cup homemade bread crumbs
    (page 141) or store-bought bread
    crumbs
3 tablespoons ketchup
1 teaspoon garlic powder
½ teaspoon salt

¼ teaspoon freshly ground pepper
About 1 tablespoon canola or other
    vegetable oil
4 ounces thinly sliced Swiss, cheddar
    or provolone cheese, cut into
    2-inch squares, optional
Baking Powder Biscuits (page 28)
Ketchup, mustard, relish, or other
    condiments, for serving

1 • In a large bowl, mix together the meat, egg, bread crumbs, ketchup, garlic powder, salt, and pepper. Form into 18 to 20 patties, each 2 inches in diameter and about ½ inch thick. The patties can be covered and refrigerated for up to 24 hours. If made from meat that has not been previously frozen, the patties can be frozen, well wrapped, for up to 2 months.

2 • Warm the oil in a skillet over medium-high heat. Brown 5 or 6 burgers (do not crowd the pan) for 4 to 5 minutes on one side, and turn. For plain burgers, cook 4 to 5 minutes on the other side, until a crust begins to form. To make cheeseburgers, place a square of cheese on each burger, cover the pan, and cook 4 to 5 minutes longer. Remove a burger from the skillet and slice in half; it should be nearly brown throughout. If it is still very pink, return it to the skillet, retesting at 3-minute intervals. Transfer the burgers to a plate and cover loosely with aluminum foil to keep warm. Repeat with remaining burgers, adding a bit more oil to the skillet between batches if the skillet seems dry.

3 • Split each biscuit and place a mini burger in between the halves. The burgers can be covered and refrigerated for up to 24 hours (wrap in aluminum foil and reheat in a 450°F oven for about 5 minutes). Transfer the burgers to a platter and serve hot, with condiments of your choice.

Makes 18 to 20 mini burgers

Sticky Spare Riblets

I humbly suggest calling these Werewolf Ribs. They're so good, they'll make you wanna howl at the moon.

5 pounds semiboneless country-style
    pork spareribs (see note), cut into
    1½ to 2-inch pieces
2 tablespoons chili powder
1 tablespoon sugar
2 teaspoons salt
1 teaspoon freshly ground pepper

4 tablespoons (½ stick) unsalted butter
⅔ cup packed light brown sugar
¼ cup Quick Barbecue Sauce
    (page 205) or store-bought
    barbecue sauce
2 tablespoons hot sauce

1 • Position a rack in the center of the oven and preheat the oven to 325°F. Using heavy-duty aluminum foil, line two 9 by 13-inch baking dishes with sides at least 1½ inches high. Divide the rib pieces among the prepared baking dishes.

2 • In a small bowl, stir together the chili powder, sugar, salt, and pepper. Sprinkle all over the rib pieces, rubbing the spices in with your fingers. Bake for 1 hour and 15 minutes, until the ribs are just beginning to brown and a good amount of fat has accumulated in the baking dishes. Remove from the oven, then drain and discard the fat.

3 • Combine the butter, brown sugar, barbecue sauce, and hot sauce in a small saucepan over medium heat, stirring until the mixture is smooth, about 3 minutes. Pour over the ribs, dividing the sauce evenly between the 2 baking dishes, and turning the ribs in the sauce to coat. Return the ribs to the oven, and bake for 1 hour and 15 minutes.

4 • Remove the baking dishes from the oven and set them on a rack to cool at least partially. The ribs are best served shortly after they are made, but they can be refrigerated, covered, for up to 2 days. (Let the ribs come to room temperature and reheat them under the broiler, or in a covered baking dish set in a preheated 400°F oven for 10 minutes.)

5 • Transfer the ribs to a platter and serve hot, warm, or at room temperature.

Makes 8 servings

NOTE: Country-style spare ribs are not actually ribs, but are cut from either the loin or the butt of the pork. Those cut from the butt end are semiboneless and work best for this recipe. Ribs cut from the loin end are boneless and can also be used in a pinch.

Chicken Fingers

It's hard to come up with a scary name for chicken fingers. My suggestion is Third Grade Teacher Fingers. That may not sound scary to you, but if you had seen my third grade teacher . . . I'm still having nightmares.

6 tablespoons canola oil or other
    vegetable oil
3 pounds boneless, skinless chicken
    breasts
2 large eggs
¼ cup whole milk
Several dashes hot sauce
1½ cups cornflake crumbs (see note)

1 teaspoon salt
1 teaspoon freshly ground pepper
½ teaspoon garlic powder
Quick Barbecue Sauce (page 205) or
    store-bought barbecue sauce,
    Mustard-Mayonnaise Sauce
    (206), ketchup, or soy sauce, for
    serving

1 • Position a rack in the center of the oven and preheat the oven to 450°F. Line a platter or baking sheet with wax paper. Divide the oil evenly between two 9 by 13-inch baking dishes with sides at least 1½ inches high.

2 • Cut the chicken breasts crosswise at a 45-degree angle into strips about 3 inches long, 1 inch wide, and ½ inch thick.

3 • In a shallow bowl, whisk together the eggs, milk, and hot sauce.

4 • In another shallow bowl, combine the cornflake crumbs, salt, pepper, and garlic powder.

5 • Dip the chicken strips into the egg mixture, then dredge them in the seasoned crumbs. Place on the prepared platter. The chicken strips can be covered and refrigerated for up to 24 hours.

6 • Place the baking dishes with the oil in the preheated oven for 5 to 7 minutes, until the oil is almost smoking. Carefully add the breaded chicken strips to the hot oil and bake for 10 minutes. Turn carefully and bake for 7 to 10 minutes more. Slice into a chicken finger to make sure it is not pink inside. If it is, return the chicken to the oven, retesting at 3-minute intervals.

7 • Transfer the chicken fingers to a warm platter. Serve with one or more dipping sauces.

Makes 8 servings

NOTE: Cornflake crumbs are available in most supermarkets, but you can also make them easily at home. Put 2 cups cornflakes cereal in a plastic bag and crush with a rolling pin, or pulse in a food processor until crushed.

Corny Crispy Rice Cereal Treats

I'm one of those people who feel there is no earthly reason why candy corn should be on this planet. It doesn't taste good, and it's colors are from no palette I'm aware of. What do I know? It's still popular. So we've taken a popular candy and a popular dessert and combined 'em to give kids and adults a new taste treat.

3 tablespoons butter	1 teaspoon pure vanilla extract
1 (10½-ounce) package miniature marshmallows	1 cup coarsely chopped candy corn
	6 cups crispy rice cereal

1 • Lightly butter a 9 by 13-inch baking pan with sides at least 1½ inches high.
2 • Melt the butter in a heavy-bottomed saucepan over low heat. Add the marshmallows and stir constantly until melted. Remove the pan from the heat and, working quickly, stir in the vanilla, then the candy corn and cereal until the cereal is well coated. Using a buttered piece of waxed paper, press the mixture into the prepared pan. Let cool completely.
3 • To serve, cut the treats into approximately 2-inch squares. The squares can be stored at room temperature in an airtight container for up to 1 week or frozen, well wrapped, for up to 1 month.

Makes twenty-four 2-inch squares

VARIATIONS

Christmas Treats

Substitute 1 cup crushed candy canes for the candy corn. (Crush the candy canes in a plastic bag using a rolling pin.)

Valentine's Day Treats

Substitute 1 cup small, heart-shaped, spicy cinnamon candies for the candy corn.

Easter Treats

Substitute 1 cup miniature jelly beans for the candy corn.

Carrot Cupcakes with Lemony Cream Cheese Frosting

Not only do these cupcakes taste great (the frosting . . . oh, the frosting) but you have less waste because they're individual baby cakes. Since the kids are already hopped up on sugar, these won't do too much more damage. If there are a couple with the frosting licked off . . . I guess you invited me to your party.

FOR THE CUPCAKES

2 large eggs
¾ cup sugar
1½ teaspoons pure vanilla extract
½ cup canola or other vegetable oil
1 cup all-purpose flour
2 teaspoons ground cinnamon
1 teaspoon baking soda
¼ teaspoon ground allspice

¼ teaspoon salt
3 large carrots, peeled and grated
   (about 2 cups)
1 (8-ounce) can crushed pineapple,
   well drained
1 cup chopped walnuts, toasted
   (page 23)

1 • Position a rack in the center of the oven and preheat the oven to 350°F. Lightly butter one standard muffin tin (2½ inch) or several mini muffin tins (2 inch), or line them with paper cupcake cups.

2 • Using an electric mixer or mixing by hand, beat together the eggs, sugar, and vanilla until light and fluffy, about 3 minutes. Add the oil in a steady stream, mixing all the while, until a thick emulsion forms. In a small bowl, stir together the flour, cinnamon, baking soda, allspice, and salt and add to the butter mixture, beating until just combined. Do not overmix. Using a spoon, stir in the carrots, pineapple, and walnuts until evenly distributed.

3 • Spoon the batter into the prepared muffins tins, filling them only three-quarters full, and bake for 25 minutes for the standard tin or 15 minutes for the mini tins. A knife inserted in the center of a cupcake should come out clean. Remove from the oven and

place on a wire rack to cool for 15 minutes. Invert the tins and remove the cupcakes, then turn them right side up. Let cool thoroughly. The cupcakes can be stored, well wrapped, at room temperature for up to 3 days or frozen for up to 2 months (thaw before proceeding).

FOR THE FROSTING

6 ounces cream cheese, softened (¾ cup)
3 tablespoons unsalted butter, softened (page 25)
¾ cup confectioners' sugar

1 tablespoon lemon juice (from 1 lemon)
¼ teaspoon pure vanilla extract

Using an electric mixer, beat together all of the ingredients. Frost the cupcakes with a flat metal spatula or a butter knife. Serve the cupcakes within 6 hours of frosting.

Makes 12 standard cupcakes or about 30 mini cupcakes

Chocolate-Chocolate Cookies

You gotta have chocolate in the Halloween sugar fest. And these cookies are frightfully good.

2½ cups semisweet chocolate chips (15 ounces)
8 tablespoons (1 stick) unsalted butter
3 large eggs
1 cup sugar
2 teaspoons pure vanilla extract

2 cups all-purpose flour
½ teaspoon baking powder
¼ teaspoon salt
2 cups old-fashioned rolled oats (not quick-cooking or instant)

1 • Melt 1½ cups of the chocolate chips with the butter in a small saucepan over medium heat, stirring until smooth. Alternatively, combine the butter and chocolate in a microwave-safe bowl, microwave on high power for 2 minutes, then stir; if the mixture is not melted, return to the microwave and cook at 30-second intervals, stirring after each interval until the mixture is smooth. Let the mixture cool.

2 • Using an electric mixer or mixing by hand, beat together the chocolate mixture with the eggs, sugar, and vanilla until smooth and shiny, about 2 minutes. In a small bowl, stir together the flour, baking powder, and salt and add to the chocolate mixture, beating just until smooth. Do not overmix. Using a spoon, stir in the oats and the remaining 1 cup chocolate chips until evenly distributed. Cover and refrigerate the batter for at least 15 minutes, and up to 24 hours.

3 • Position 2 racks equidistant apart in the oven. Preheat the oven to 350°F. Lightly butter 2 cookie sheets, or line them with parchment paper.

4 • Scoop 2 tablespoons of cookie dough at a time, rolling each scoop into a ball. Place the balls of dough 1½ inches apart on the prepared sheets. The balls of dough can be covered and frozen for several hours until firm, then transferred to an airtight container and frozen for up to 1 month.

5 • Bake the cookies for 8 to 10 minutes (1 or 2 minutes more if frozen), switching the position of the baking sheets halfway through the baking time, until the cookies begin to look dry and a bit cracked on top. Remove from the oven and let the cookies sit on the

baking sheets for about 2 minutes. Using a metal spatula, transfer the cookies to a wire rack to cool.

6 • Repeat with the remaining dough, making sure you let the baking sheets cool completely before proceeding.

7 • The cookies can be stored at room temperature in an airtight container for up to 1 week or frozen, well wrapped, for up to 2 months (thaw before serving).

Makes 30 cookies

Caramel Apples

I was given a bribe by the American Dental Association to include this recipe. I'm kidding. Just a joke. Growing up, we had candied apples with a deep red hard candy shell. It was like a lollipop with an apple inside.

These are softer and gooier and messier. So put a tarp down on the floor and serve 'em up.

1 (14-ounce) bag caramels, unwrapped	1 tablespoon pure vanilla extract
1 tablespoon heavy or light cream or half-and-half	8 small red apples (about 2 pounds), washed, dried, and stemmed

1 • Line a baking sheet with wax paper and generously butter the wax paper.

2 • In a double boiler, combine the caramels and cream and cook, stirring occasionally, until the caramels are melted and the mixture is smooth. Stir in the vanilla.

3 • Skewer the stem end of each apple with a Popsicle stick or a chopstick. Dip the apples, one at a time, into the melted caramel, using a table knife to smooth the coating on the apples. You want to cover at least three-quarters of each apple. As they are done, place them, stick up, on the prepared baking sheet. Let sit for at least 15 minutes, so that the coating can cool and become firm.

4 • The apples can be kept, uncovered, at room temperature for 24 hours, but if you live in a humid climate, they are best served soon after they are made.

Makes 8 apples

VARIATION

Nutty Caramel Apples

While still warm, dip the bottom of the apples into 1 cup chopped toasted pecans (page 23) or other nuts.

Holiday Hotlines and Helpful Web Sites

Many of the following hotlines and consumer lines have live operators to help you diffuse your holiday kitchen crises and answer cooking questions. Some are available year-round, seven days a week; others are seasonal (November and December) and some are available only on weekdays during standard business hours. You'll also find some Web sites here (open all night!), just in case.

BETTY CROCKER

888-ASK-BETTY

www.bettycrocker.com

BUTTERBALL TURKEY TALK-LINE

800-BUTTERBALL

www.butterball.com

COOK'S ILLUSTRATED MAGAZINE

www.turkeyhelp.com

EMPIRE KOSHER POULTRY CUSTOMER HOTLINE

800-367-4734

www.empirekosher.com

FOSTER FARMS TURKEY HELPLINE

800-255-7227

www.fosterfarms.com

LAND O'LAKES

www.landolakes.com

NATIONAL TURKEY FEDERATION

www.eatturkey.com

NESTLE TOLL HOUSE BAKING INFORMATION LINE

800-637-8537

www.verybestbaking.com

OCEAN SPRAY CONSUMER HELPLINE

800-662-3263

www.oceanspray.com

PERDUE

800-473-7383

www.perdue.com

PILLSBURY

www.pillsbury.com

REYNOLDS TURKEY TIPS LINE

800-745-4000

www.reynoldskitchens.com

U.S. DEPARTMENT OF AGRICULTURE MEAT AND POULTRY HOTLINE

800-535-4555

www.fsis.usda.gov

Sources

BAKING SUPPLIES

CHEF'S CATALOGUE

800-884-2433

PENZEY'S SPICES

800-741-7787

www.penzeys.com

THE KING ARTHUR FLOUR BAKER'S CATALOGUE

800-827-6836

www.kingarthurflour.com

SPECIALTY MEATS

ALLEN BROTHERS

3737 SOUTH HALSTEAD STREET

CHICAGO, IL 60609–1689

800-957-0111

GEORGETOWN FARM

BOX 558, RR1, BOX 14W

MADISON, VA 22724

540-948-4209

NIMAN RANCH

1025 EAST 12TH STREET

OAKLAND, CA 94606

510-808-0330

www.nimanranch.com

SPECIALTY SEAFOOD

BROWNE TRADING COMPANY

MERRILL'S WHARF

260 COMMERCIAL STREET

PORTLAND, ME 04101

800-944-7848

www.brownetrading.com

fresh seafood, smoked fish, caviar

KATY'S SMOKEHOUSE

707-677-0151

www.katyssmokehouse.com

fresh and smoked seafood

SPECIALTY FOODS, CONDIMENTS, & SAUCES

AMERICAN SPOON FOODS

800-222-5886

www.spoon.com

preserves, sauces, butters, dressings

DEAN & DELUCA

2526 EAST 36TH ST. NORTH CIRCLE

WICHITA, KS 67219

877-826-9246

www.deandeluca.com

preserves, condiments, dressings,
prepared foods

STONEWALL KITCHEN

800-207-5267

www.stonewallkitchen.com

preserves, condiments, dressings,
prepared foods

THE LEE BROTHERS BOILED PEANUTS CATALOGUE

843-720-8890

www.boiledpeanuts.com

Southern regional foods

TABLEWARE AND BARWARE

CRATE & BARREL

800-967-6696

www.crateandbarrel.com

POTTERY BARN

888-779-5176

www.potterybarn.com

WILLIAMS-SONOMA

800-840-2591

www.williams-sonoma.com

PARTY SUPPLIES

IPARTY

800-447-2789

www.iparty.com

ORIENTAL TRADING COMPANY

800-875-8480

www.oriental.com

PARTY SUPPLIES SHOP

866-272-9897

www.partysuppliesshop.com

Index